ANGELS OUR FRIEND

SAYANI BOSE

Contents

Disclaimer

Protected by copyright law. No piece of this book might be recreated by any mechanical, visual, or electronic cycle, or as phonographic recording; nor may it be put away in a recovery framework, sent, or on the other hand in any case be replicated for public or confidential use —other than for "fair use" as brief citations typified in articles and surveys — without earlier composed, consent of the distributer.

The writer of this book doesn't apportion clinical counsel or endorse the utilization of any strategy as a type of therapy for physical, profound, or clinical issues without the guidance of a doctor, either straight forwardly or in a roundabout way. The expectation of the creator is just to offer data of an overall sort to help you in your journey for close to home and profound prosperity. In the occasion you utilize any of the data in this book for yourself, which is your established right, the author and publisher assume no responsibility for your action.

Contents

Introduction

Who Are The ANGELS?

In different mystical strict customs a holy messenger is an extraordinary otherworldly being who serves God.

Abrahamic religions frequently portray holy messengers as generous divine go-betweens between God (or Heaven) and mankind. Different jobs incorporate defenders and guides for people, and workers of God. Abrahamic religions depict heavenly orders, which change by religion and group. A few holy messengers have explicit names (like Gabriel or Michael) or titles (like seraph or lead celestial host). Those ousted from Heaven are called fallen heavenly messengers, unmistakable from the magnificent host.

Holy messengers in craftsmanship are typically molded like people of uncommon magnificence. They are many times recognized in Christian craftsmanship with bird wings, radiances, and heavenly light.The word holy messenger shows up in present day English from Old English engel (with a hard g) and the Old French angele.Both of these get from Late Latin angelus, which thus was acquired from Late Greek angelos (in a real sense "courier"). The word's earliest structure is Mycenaean a-ke-ro, verified in Linear B syllabic content. As indicated by the Dutch etymologist R. S. P. Beekes, angelos itself might be "an Oriental credit, as (angaros, 'Persian mounted courier')."

The delivering of "angelos" is the Septuagint's default interpretation of the Biblical Hebrew term malakh, meaning basically "courier" without indicating its tendency. In the Latin Vulgate, this importance becomes bifurcated: when malkh or angelos should signify a human courier, words like nuntaius or legatus are applied. Assuming that the word alludes to some heavenly being, the word angelus shows up. Such separation has been taken over by later vernacular interpretations of the Bible, early Christian and Jewish exegetes and in the end current scholars.In Zoroastrianism there are different heavenly messenger like figures. For instance, every individual has one heavenly messenger, called Fravashi. They belittle people and different animals, and furthermore manifest God's energy. The Amesha Spentas have frequently been viewed as heavenly messengers, despite the fact that there is no immediate reference to them passing on messages,but are fairly radiations of Ahura Mazda ("Wise Lord", God); they at first showed up in a theoretical design and afterward became customized, related with different parts of creation.In Judaism, heavenly messengers (Hebrew: "courier"), are perceived through translation of the Tanakh and in a long practice as extraordinary creatures who stand by God in paradise, however are rigorously to be recognized from God (YHWH) and are subordinate to him. Periodically, they can show chosen individuals God's will and instructions.In the Jewish practice they are additionally substandard compared to people since they have no will of their own and can complete just a single heavenly order.

Hebrew Bible

Three heavenly messengers facilitated by Abraham, Ludovico Carracci (c. 1610-1612), Bologna, Pinacoteca Nazionale

Tobias and the Angel by Filippino Lippi, made between c. 1472 and c. 1482

The Torah utilizes the Hebrew expressions "courier of God"),("courier of the Lord"), ("children of God") and "the heavenly ones") to allude to creatures generally deciphered as holy messengers. Later texts utilize different terms, for example, "the upper ones").

The term is additionally utilized in different books of the Hebrew Bible. Contingent upon the unique circumstance, the Hebrew word might allude to a human courier or to a heavenly courier. A human courier may be a prophet or minister, like Malachi, "my courier"; the Greek superscription in the Septuagint interpretation expresses the Book of Malachi was stated "by the hand of his courier". Instances of an otherworldly courier are the "Malak YHWH," who is either a courier from God, a part of God, (for example, the logos),or God himself as the courier (the "theophanic holy messenger.")

Michael D. Coogan noticed that it is just in the late books that the expressions "come to mean the kind semi-divine creatures natural from later folklore and craftsmanship." Daniel is the scriptural book to allude to individual heavenly messengers by name, referencing Gabriel in Daniel 9:21 and Michael in Daniel 10:13. These holy messengers are essential for Daniel's prophetically catastrophic dreams and are a significant piece of whole-world destroying writing.

In Daniel 7, Daniel gets a fantasy vision from God. As Daniel watches, the Ancient of Days sits down on the privileged position of paradise and sits in judgment amidst the sublime court a [angel] like a child of man moves toward the Ancient One in the billows of paradise and is given never-ending majesty.

Coogan makes sense of the improvement of this idea of holy messengers: "In the postexilic period, with the improvement of unequivocal monotheism, these heavenly creatures — the 'children of God' who were individuals from the Divine Council — were active downgraded to what are currently known as 'heavenly messengers', comprehended as creatures made by God, however eternal and subsequently better than people." This origination of heavenly messengers is best grasped as opposed to devils and is many times remembered to be "impacted by the old Persian strict practice of Zoroastrianism, which saw the world as a milestone between powers of good and powers of malevolence, among light and haziness." One of these is, a figure portrayed in (among different spots) the Book of Job.

Rabbinic Judaism

As per Rabbinic Judaism, the holy messengers have no bodies, however are interminably living animals made out of fire. The Babylonian Talmud peruses as "The Torah was not given to serving heavenly messengers." typically comprehended as an admission to human's defect, as opposed to the holy messengers. Subsequently, they sporadically show up in Midrashim as contest with humans.The holy messengers as radiant creatures, stringently adhering to the laws of God, become envious of God's friendship for man. People, by following the Torah, in petition, by opposing detestable senses and by teshuva, are liked to the immaculate holy messengers. Thus, they are additionally substandard compared to people in the Jewish practice. In the Midrash, the plural of El (Elohim) utilized in Genesis comparable to the formation of people is made sense of by the presence of heavenly messengers: God hence talked with the heavenly messengers, yet settled on the last choice alone. This story fills in for instance, instructing that the strong ought to likewise talk with the feeble. God's own official choice features God's undisputable transcendence.

In post-Biblical Judaism,[clarification needed] certain holy messengers took on specific importance and created extraordinary characters and jobs. Albeit these lead celestial hosts were accepted to rank among the eminent host, no orderly progressive system at any point created. Metatron is viewed as one of the greatest of the holy messengers in Merkabah and Kabbalah magic and frequently fills in as a copyist; he is momentarily referenced in the Talmud and figures conspicuously in Merkabah supernatural texts. Michael, who fills in as a champion and backer for Israel,(Daniel 10:13) is viewed especially affectionately. Gabriel is referenced in the Book of Daniel (Daniel 8:15-17) and momentarily in the Talmud, as well as in numerous Merkabah enchanted texts. There is no proof in Judaism for the love of holy messengers, however there is proof for the summon and in some cases even conjuration of heavenly messengers.

Philo of Alexandria distinguishes the holy messenger with the Logos in light of the fact that the holy messenger is the unimportant voice of God. The holy messenger is something else from God himself, yet is considered as God's instrument.

Four classes of serving holy messengers serve and complete recognition before the Holy One, favored be He: the principal camp (drove by) Michael to His right side, the subsequent camp (drove by) Gabriel to His left side, the third camp (drove by) Uriel before Him, and the fourth camp (drove by) Raphael behind Him; and the Shekhinah of the Holy One, favored be He, is in the middle. He is perched on a lofty position high and magnified.

Confidence in holy messengers is basic to Islam. The Quranic word for holy messenger gets either from Malaka, signifying "he controlled", because of their ability to oversee various issues doled out to them, or from the root either from '-l-k, l-'-k or m-l-k with the wide significance of a "courier", very much like its partners in Hebrew (malakh) and Greek (angelos). Not at all like their Hebrew partner, the term is solely utilized for eminent spirits of the heavenly world, however not really for human couriers. The Quran alludes to both radiant and human couriers as "rasul" instead.Contrary to mainstream thinking, heavenly messengers are never depicted as specialists of disclosure in the Quran, in spite of the fact that translation credits Gabriel with that.

The Quran is the chief hotspot for the Islamic idea of angels.Some of them, like Gabriel and Michael, are referenced by name in the Quran, others are simply alluded to by their capability. In hadith writing, holy messengers are frequently doled out to just a single explicit phenomena.Angels assume a huge part in Mi'raj writing, where Muhammad experiences a few holy messengers during his excursion through the heavens.Further holy messengers have frequently been highlighted in Islamic eschatology, Islamic philosophy and Islamic philosophy.Duties relegated to heavenly messengers incorporate, for instance, conveying divine revelations, commending God, recording each individual's activities, and taking an individual's spirit at the hour of death.

In Islam, very much like in Judaism and Christianity, heavenly messengers are many times addressed in human structures joined with powerful pictures, like wings, being of extraordinary size or wearing eminent articles.The

Quran portrays them as "couriers with wings — two, or three, or four: He [God] adds to Creation as He pleases..."Common attributes for heavenly messengers are their missing requirements for substantial cravings, like eating and drinking.Their absence of proclivity to material longings is additionally communicated by their creation from light: Angels of kindness are made from nur (cold light) contrary to the holy messengers of discipline made from nar (hot light).Muslims don't for the most part share the view of celestial pictorial portrayals, like those tracked down in Western workmanship.

Despite the fact that trusting in holy messengers stay one of Six Articles of Faith in Islam, one can not track down an opinionated angelology in Islamic custom. In spite of this, researchers played examined the part of heavenly messengers from explicit accepted occasions, like the Mi'raj, and Quranic sections. Regardless of whether they are not in center, they have been highlighted in legends, theory discusses and deliberate philosophy. While in old style Islam, far and wide ideas were acknowledged as sanctioned, there is a tendecy in contemporary grant to dismiss a lot of material about heavenly messengers, such as calling the Angel of Death by the name Azra'il.

In Folk Islam, individual heavenly messengers might be evoked in expulsion customs, whose names are engraved in charms or amulets.

A few present day researchers have underscored a figurative reevaluation of the idea of angels.

CHAPTER ONE

Does angels connect with us :

Angels. Heavenly messengers. The very word evokes mental symbolism of clear creatures appended to wings. In any case, are heavenly messengers genuine?

Yes angels are genuine.That is on the grounds that there exists a convergence between human otherworldliness and general brain research.

My guru my teacher who heals and taught me with angel therapy, clarified for me that while the term holy messenger may abstract, its importance is universal. Heres the way in which she characterizes a heavenly messenger. Your definition might be something very similar.

A courier from a more powerful that some call God. Heavenly messengers are shipped off guide us and show significant life illustrations. Angelsspeak to us every day.Charmed, I requested that she let me know more. What my guru shared was fascinating!In truth, I was so found her understanding that I chose to jotit all down.

Some of the stunning ways holy messengers address us consistently.

Holy messengers regularly come to you in your fantasies, however you may not remember them or recollect the fantasies after waking. To increase your familiarity with dream time correspondences from your heavenly messengers, put shortly addressing your heavenly messengers before you fall asleep.

Request that your holy messengers visit you in your fantasies and offer significant experiences that you might have to be aware. Keep a note pad and pen by your bed, and after waking attempt to review your fantasies. Write down any subtleties you can recall, regardless of whether they appear to be connected with heavenly messengers

Over the long run, you might begin getting messages from your holy messengers while you dream, and you will work on your capacity to review anything of significance.

For instance, assuming you have been dreaming about somebody with earthy colored eyes, it very well might be a message from past that proposes you want to become hotter and more open to somebody you love.

In some cases your heavenly messengers will attempt to certainly stand out through actual sensations like shivering, a sensation of warmth spreading over you, a light touch on your hand, a sensation of somebody tenderly stroking your hair, or even a substantial presence in the room with you.

This frequently happens when you are scared or miserable about something and your holy messengers need to comfort you. At the point when you feel sensations like these, make certain to recognize them.

Say, "Thank you heavenly messengers, I can feel you here with me and I'm appreciative for your affection and backing."

Your holy messengers may likewise convey in additional conspicuous ways, such as talking straightforwardly to you. You might hear a voice, either inside your head or a voice that appears to come from beyond you, in any event, when no other person is near.

All the time this will happen when your heavenly messengers need to share an indispensable data to guard you. They might make statements like, "Comply with as far as possible," or "Don't take the turnpike today." This sort of correspondence can be challenging to accept on occasion.

You might contemplate whether you are simply envisioning the voice, and you might try and be enticed to excuse it. Regardless of whether you feel a little doubtful about whether your heavenly messengers are truly addressing you, it's really smart to heed the guidance you hear on the grounds that more often than not it will assist you with staying away from a few horrendous encounters.

Heavenly messengers can likewise speak with different sounds other than voices. You might hear faint vocalizations that sound like heavenly messengers singing, delicate ringers tolling, or music with no evident source. At the point when this occurs, recognize it and request that your holy messengers make it more clear.

You could express something like this: "Holy messengers, I assume I hear you, yet entirely it's actual weak. Might you at any point make it somewhat stronger?" Then sit unobtrusively and concentrate, and most frequently you will actually want to tune in better.

In the event that you are a visual individual, you might see mental dreams while reflecting or as of now before you nod off. You might see whirling tones, shimmers of light, or even an unmistakable picture of one of your holy messengers remaining before you.

It is likewise conceivable to see visual peculiarities in your environmental elements as you approach your day to day daily schedule. You might see little glimmers or dashes of light, or catch a fast look at a shining figure that seems to be a holy messenger, however it vanishes when you go to gaze straight toward it

This typically implies that you are turning out to be more delicate to the presence of your holy messengers. They are dependably around you, however you might not have been tuned adequately in to see it previously.

Your holy messengers may likewise convey by offering you hints or images over the course of the day. These signs can change generally, and they will typically be extremely private to you.

A few models may be finding white plumes any place you go; seeing a guard sticker that peruses, "You Are Loved" right when you really wanted such an update; or an ideal bloom filling in a spot you least anticipated it.

The most effective way to tell whether these encounters are genuinely signs from your heavenly messengers or simple fortuitous event is to focus on how you feel. A sign from your holy messengers will continuously have an unmistakable inclination connected to it, similar to an uplifted feeling of mindfulness or an overwhelming inclination that somebody is attempting to let you know something.

Holy messengers can likewise speak with you through human or creature "aides". For instance, you could ask your heavenly messengers for guidance on a specific subject before you go to work, and afterward one of your colleagues will express the specific words you expected to hear

Or on the other hand you could see a creature in nature and it appears to catch your eye emphatically, so you'll look into the imagery of that creature and find that it holds importance for you.

Your heavenly messengers can speak with you in vast ways, however the key is to focus essentially. The more you work on elevating your familiarity with your heavenly messengers and following the bits of knowledge and hunches you get from them, you will turn out to be considerably more certain about knowing when your heavenly messengers are attempting to stand out.

CHAPTER TWO

Our heavenly messengers routinely give us messages. For our purposes, heavenly messengers' signs and signals are at times not generally simple to see and perceive. For us individuals, it very well may be hard to see them because of the hecticness of daily existence. Hence, the heavenly messengers frequently send us similar messages they have for us a few times, trusting that they can assist us with that. In this article, I might want to educate you seriously regarding what characters happen with the goal that you can all the more likely perceive the heavenly messenger characters.

How do the heavenly messengers offer us hints and signals?

Holy messengers frequently give us their messages in an unobtrusive manner, through little things that we experience on our way. Of which we frequently think: "Hello, that is an occurrence" or "no, I'll presumably make it up myself." You likely believed that when you ran over something that 'nearly' seemed to be a sign. Furthermore, with that, nearly I don't mean in a real sense that it nearly seemed to be, yet particularly that it was likely a sign! A sign that your head thusly utilized. So know that the holy messengers offer us hints through various channels. There's nothing that their signs can't be, I have portrayed a couple underneath.

What heavenly messenger characters are there:

I just said darlings offer us their hints in a wide range of various ways. It might be that you get a sign that isn't recorded underneath; there is basically no standard for how the heavenly messengers do that. Be that as it may, underneath are the manners in which the holy messengers frequently use.

Feathers on your way

Heavenly messengers are known for their quills. Spring on your way can mean various things. It might say that the holy messengers need to let you know something or that they need to tell you that they are with you. Your divine messenger can tell you that the person is there, coordinating your affection and looking after you. A quill from your holy messenger may likewise need to let you know something different. Frequently you know naturally what this is, yet our psyche brimming with considerations frequently clears out this inclination before it has the opportunity to come up.

Through heavenly messengers numbers

Do you routinely awaken around midnight and see a similar time on your morning timer? Or on the other hand each time you take a gander at your telephone, you see a similar time once more, for instance, 18:18 or 22:22. At the point when these numbers continue to return to you, your heavenly messenger needs to give you something. You can find more about the importance of holy messenger numbers on this page: Angel numbers and their motivations.

By means of human couriers

Heavenly messengers can likewise tell us something through human couriers. These are many times individuals we scarcely know or know by any means, however now and again even through colleagues of us. Normally they give you something that you will be quiet about thereafter, on the grounds that you thoroughly don't expect that individual can offer something altogether fitting for that second in your life.

Individual model

I personally have a fantastic illustration of this: where I stay individuals routinely come running past my kitchen window and nursery. At the point when I escaped my nursery door and strolled up the barrier to my vehicle, a woman approached me, I had seen her pass by commonly, and we generally expressed farewell to one another. I actually have no clue about what her name was, and I never told her my name by the same token. (there is likewise no name on our entryway, just a house number) She came to me while I needed to get in my vehicle and in a real sense congratulated me. She said that I did really amazing work and that I needed to keep it up. I just said 'thank you' in shock, and she strolled on.

My own head likewise attempts to consider a wide range of coherent explanations behind this, yet my instinct offered something else entirely at that point! There are numerous manners by which heavenly messengers send human couriers to us, through associates or through outsiders who are mysteriously gone subsequent to telling their message. Be available to it and get these caring messages!

I would like to add more on my personal experience. When I got to sleep and lay on my bed most of the time I felt soothing smell around me. My body feels a sensation and most of the time I felt someone is there around me and sitting on my bed. It gives me a goosebumps but it feels heavenly.

Mists

Heavenly messengers can likewise tell us through the mists that they are there. Through mists through something essential to you at that point, or in the method of a heavenly messenger. Also, remember the sun's beams with all their light and warmth. At the point when a delightful light emission sparkles right at the spot that is huge or significant to you, it can likewise be an indication of your heavenly messenger.

Texts and words

You most likely remember it, you drive or cycle some place for quite a while, and out of nowhere you notice a word or entry composed some place. It quickly gives you mental fortitude and strength at that point of perusing, and you feel the energy moving through your body. Holy messengers are novel and astounding animals; they let you in on things in a wide range of ways. So when you run over a message that appears to you at that point, thank your heavenly messengers for sending their adoration!

To dream

My heavenly messengers consistently give me things through my viewpoints. At the point when we are snoozing, the holy messengers can contact us all the more rapidly on the grounds that we are not in our minds. We are associated with the holy messengers around us during our rest.

At the point when your divine messenger gives you something through your fantasy, then it is much of the time an unmistakable message and a reasonable message. At the point when you promptly know when you awaken that it was a specific dream, that it was a message, take it from your sentiments. It is hard to verbalize how instinct functions, yet you simply know naturally when it is.

Remember that during the day, your head is given opportunity to reach out and future time up with a wide range of clarifications. At the point when you are simply conscious, and you awaken feeling it was a message, trust it. At the point when you are simply alert, you are more associated with your holy messengers and your heart than around mid-afternoon. (Not that we are not associated with the holy messengers around mid-afternoon, but since of the issues of the day, we frequently don't see this.) Therefore, trust yourself and your instinct.

It is likewise a fact that when you have had a celestial dream, you can in any case recall those days after the fact well, while you frequently forget 'typical' dreams. I, when all is said and done, can recollect my saintly dreams from quite a while back to the current day.

Motivation and boldness

At the point when you unexpectedly get motivation or boldness for something you are doing or are doing, thank your divine messenger! Frequently this happens when we let go of it briefly and don't intentionally consider it. Your divine messenger needs to help and guide you on your way of life. They do this by sending you boldness or motivation. You know it; unexpectedly you feel the energy streaming once more. Or on the other hand abruptly you understand what to do or have an astounding thought that makes your heart sing. At the point when you feel that your energy is going up, the thought makes you blissful and gives you boldness once more, then, at that point, expect that it is great. It is a thought of the heavenly messengers around you, set out to take the plunge.

Your heavenly messenger knows your life way, understands what your examples are on this planet. At the point when you get heavenly motivation, take it with two hands!

The Rainbow

Heavenly messengers additionally let them in on that they are with you through rainbows. At the point when a rainbow out of the blue appears to you, and it seems like it is for you at that point, believe that!

Now and again everything appears to be obvious, you have the breeze down metaphorically! It is an incredible inclination on the off chance that everything is correct. This frequently happens when you are in good shape and accomplish something that is essential for your life's motivation. And negative, that doesn't imply that everything goes without a hitch and you can simply take a load off, yet over all that entryways continue to open for you, it moves along as expected, and you feel better. Your heavenly messenger couldn't want anything more than to assist you with tracking down your way. At the point when you are in good shape, they might tell you by opening entryways for you. It then appears as though they open for you naturally. Know then that your heavenly messengers behind the scenes have been buckling down for you!

How do you have at least some idea everything the heavenly messengers need to say to you about their signs and messages?

Everybody can perceive the indications of their holy messengers. What's more, everybody gets signs from the holy messengers. How do you have at least some idea everything that they need to say to you? Furthermore, how can you say whether it is a sign? Characters from the holy messengers are in every case brimming with cherishing energy. At the point when you get a sign or sign from your heavenly messenger, that's what you know. Your instinct frequently lets you know this following getting it. Following a couple of moments, your head will take over in the future. Know about this. By realizing that your instinct can be felt right away, however before you can frequently feel it being shouted through your head once more, you can consider this. Know about this!

Your head is great at weakening signs

At the point when your head assumes control over, attempt to return to the inclination that originally sprung up in you! That is your instinct! Assuming you feel instinctive 'indeed, that is a message' or 'indeed, this is a sign!', Trust that regardless, your head comes later. Your head is great at discrediting your confidence in the sign with considerations, for example, "indeed, I make it up myself" or "I simply need to feel that myself."

As I recently expressed, indications of holy messengers are constantly centered around aiding you. Heavenly messengers likewise never talk from the 'I' structure, however consistently from 'we.' Angel characters are continuously adoring. You feel reinforced by a sign after their message. You feel certainty develop. At the point when you experience this inclination through, for instance, a word on your way or a plume on your way, you realize that they are your holy messengers. Trust yourself and your instinct. Everything the heavenly messengers need to say to you, naturally, frequently comes through rapidly! You then know without thinking what the sign is for. You feel and understand what it is really going after.

hints to understand all the more likely perceive holy messenger signs and signals:

I know and see very well that getting the signs from your angels isn't simple all the time. With these tips, I desire to help you on your way.

Hints 1: Ask for explicit signals or signs

The inquiry: "Dear holy messengers, if it's not too much trouble, help me" isn't quite certain. The assist you with getting can be anything. To get a sign by means of a quill, request a plume. For instance, pose the inquiry: Dear divine messenger, let me know through a spring on my way that I am in good shape. If you have any desire to get motivation before I notice something: composing a blog entry. Then request motivation for a blog entry. Be clear, and you will get lucidity.

Hints 2: Meditate

Reflecting assists you with associating more with yourself and your heart. At the point when you are more associated with your inward world, it becomes simpler to trust your instinct. At the point when you trust your instinct, you are more open to the indications of your heavenly messengers. Reflection likewise assists you with quieting your flood of contemplations; this additionally assists you with getting radiant characters.

Hints 3: Earthing

At the point when you are appropriately grounded, you stay with yourself more. You are firmer from your perspective. You are more associated with yourself and everything around you. Also, with your heavenly messengers. At the point when you are appropriately grounded, you float somewhat less in the issues of the day, in your flood of contemplations, or in the materialistic world. You return to yourself and your sentiments. You can likewise feel better what feels much better and what isn't. What comes from your heavenly messengers and what doesn't.

Hints 4: Look around with consideration

Life is occupied nowadays, and there are a wide range of interruptions around us. In some cases we stroll around like a chicken without a head or go around prior. This makes it harder for your holy messengers to contact you. Assuming you are so occupied or diverted, you frequently don't see the signs that the holy messengers give you. Then, at that point, assume a pass in position. Switch off your telephone one evening, go into nature, and be astounded. Then, at that point, look with consideration around you, you will see that there are such countless surprisingly marvels around you!

Hints 5: Ask your holy messengers for help

Ask your holy messengers for help to make you more responsive to their signs. You can likewise inquire as to whether they need to help instinct. Ask such that feels right to you. Resoundingly or as a main priority. Keep in mind, holy messengers are anxious to help you, however endlessly doing whatever it may take to further develop your instinct really depends on you.

Begin and ask your holy messengers for signs!

Holy messengers are eager to assist you; it depends on you to perceive their assistance and to accomplish something with it! Begin and don't surrender in the event that it doesn't work immediately. Give it a few time and give yourself some time. Trust yourself and the heavenly messengers around you. Furthermore, recall when you miss a sign, your heavenly messengers offer their hints on different occasions until you notice them. I trust this article has helped you and that it might help you. how would I know my heavenly messenger is with me

How might you perceive a message through a fantasy of your heavenly messengers..

There are many ways of thinking with regards to the quantity of chief heavenly messengers which exist, each addressed by their own fanciful importance and history. A few notable lead celestial hosts show up in the writing and masterpieces delivered by differing conviction frameworks and societies, and are remembered for such mediums across ranges of time.

Otherworldly guide Radleigh Valentine recommends that every one of us has no less than two divine messengers alloted to us upon entering the world to pay special attention to our individual physical, mental, and close to home prosperity. Our domain of presence in this lifetime is made out of a few components which are consistently changing and cooperating in show (think earth, air, water, fire); inside our singular vessels a comparative science unfurls on a more limited size. Similarly as the lead celestial hosts arrange components, they can go about as guides for individuals when called upon.

Do you know the names of heavenly messengers in the Bible and their obligations? The Holy Book Doesn't demonstrate the number of heavenly messengers that exist, however each plays a plainly characterized part. Heavenly messengers will be couriers of God, and their work is to convey alerts, decipher dreams, and issue decrees. However, these magnificent animals are additionally instruments of God's will. They lead God's will on the planet and are dynamic in the ordered progression of occasions alluded to as the finish of times.

While the Bible notices heavenly messengers on many events, their singular names are referenced a couple of times. Furthermore, only one out of every odd heavenly messenger is referenced by name in the Bible. Here is a rundown of 15 names of holy messengers in the good book and their obligations separately.

Chief heavenly messenger Michael

Known as the most impressive of the lead celestial hosts, Michael is generally viewed as an incredible defender of physical, mental, and close to home wellness as well as material belongings.

Michael can be called upon as a wellspring of solidarity, direction, and delivery when one is feeling unfortunate and deceived.

Addressed by the component of fire, Michael aids the evacuation of fiery blockages, crafted by Michael can control people toward their deep yearnings and reason.

Michael is among the rundown of holy messengers in paradise who has a higher positioning than the rest. The Bible alludes to him as the main sovereign of the glorious.

Heavenly messenger Samael

He is considered in Midrashic texts to be an individual from the great host with frequently dreary and damaging obligations. Perhaps of Samael's most prominent job in Jewish legend is that of the principal holy messenger of death and the head of satans. In spite of the fact that he overlooks the wrongdoings of man, he stays one of God's workers. He shows up habitually in the narrative of Garden of Eden and designed the fall of Adam and Eve with a snake in works during the Second Temple period. However, the snake isn't a type of Samael, yet a monster he rode like a camel. In a solitary record he is additionally accepted to be the dad of Cain, as well as the accomplice of Lilith. In early Talmudic and Midrashic writing he isn't related to Satan yet. Just in later Midrashim he is named "top of all the satans".

As divine messenger and sovereign of Rome, he is the chief rival of Israel. By the start of Jewish culture in Europe, Samael had been laid out as a delegate of Christianity, because of his relationship with Rome.

In a few Gnostic cosmologies, Samael's job as wellspring of evil became related to the Demiurge, the maker of the material world. Albeit likely the two records start from a similar source, the Gnostic improvement contrasts from the Jewish advancement of Samael, in which Samael is only a heavenly messenger and worker of God.

Archangel Raguel

Raguel is quite often alluded to as the lead celestial host of equity, reasonableness, congruity, retaliation, and reclamation. He is likewise in some cases known as the lead celestial host of speech. Raguel is one of the seven heavenly messengers whose job is to watch. His number is 6, and his capability is to get revenge on the universe of the lights who have violated God's laws.

Raguel's obligations have continued as before across Jewish and Christian practices. Similar as a sheriff or constable, Raguel's motivation has forever been to hold fallen heavenly messengers and devils within proper limits, conveying judgment upon any that over-step their limits. He has been known to annihilate underhanded spirits and cast fallen holy messengers into Hell (called Gehenna in the Hebrew Old Testament and called Tartarus in the Greek New Testament).

Raguel isn't referenced in the authoritative works of the Bible. Notwithstanding, in 2 Enoch, which is for the most part thought to be non-standard, the patriarch Enoch was conveyed as a human to and from Heaven by the holy messengers Raguel and Sariel.

Conceivable verifiable references to a comparative figure from different societies can be tracked down in Babylonian culture as "Cloth" (a few interpretations say Ragumu), and in Sumerian as "Apparatus" and that means to talk or discourse. In this way, these comparable characters addressed balance in those societies too.

Lead celestial host Raphael

A specialist of mending, Raphael has long filled in as a hotspot for those looking for physical, mental, and close to home stronghold later and during encountering injury, compulsion, and unevenness; this lead celestial host is likewise an aide for those offering recuperating administrations expertly from specialists to specialists to educators of yoga and reflection. Raphael looks out for voyagers, guaranteeing smooth changes and security throughout the span of one's excursions.

Rather fittingly, this heavenly being is frequently connected with the component of air; Raphael can assist those looking for his direction with discovering a feeling of softness and lucidity, and lay preparation for reestablishing dependability.

Whether it be returning to the actual body or a geographic area, Raphael guarantees those mentioning his presence get back. Raphael is among the high-positioning lead celestial hosts in the rundown of names of holy messengers in paradise and their obligations. He remains before the lofty position of the Lord. A portion of his obligations incorporate introducing the requests of the holy people and going into the presence of the brilliance of God. It is additionally his work to mend the earth debased by the fallen holy messengers. The name Raphael implies God mends.

Lead celestial host Gabriel

This lead celestial host fills in as a scaffold to grasping among self and self, and self and others. Gabriel is perceived in numerous practices as the female partner to Michael with regards to rank.

As the benefactor of correspondence, Gabriel is an asset of motivation and assists with nullifying lingering and delay propensities, which can become blocks for individual articulation and instinct.

The evacuation of such obstructions considers those requesting Gabriel's guide to lower themselves in the progression of encountering, accounting for fruitfulness in the entirety of its structures: imagination, youngster raising and - bearing, and guardian overflow. The chief heavenly messenger connected with the component of water, the wellspring of all life, guarantees that those appealing to for help easily float through their undertakings as opposed to suffocate in overpower. The name Gabriel implies God is my solidarity. He is one of a handful of the holy messengers referenced in the Scriptures by name whose service is by all accounts that of commitment and benevolence. The main job he played was conveying the fresh insight about the approaching of Jesus. The Bible likewise depicts him as the heavenly messenger.

Lead celestial host Uriel

Uriel is a heavenly messenger of shrewdness. He is a lead celestial host who looks after thunder and fear. In current Christianity, Uriel is a holy messenger of the heavenly presence, contrition, and lead celestial host of salvation. Christians portray him conveying a book or a papyrus look over that addresses insight. In early Christian fanciful books, he protects St. John the Baptist from Herod's slaughter of the honest people. Uriel implies God is my Light.

Lead celestial host Azrael

Azrael holds the job of the heavenly messenger of death. He is answerable for moving the departed's spirit after death and assisting them with disconnecting from the actual body as they enter their next period of life. Being the heavenly messenger of death doesn't mean Azrael causes demise. All things being equal, he helps those lamenting the deficiency of their friends and family to get solace.

Lead celestial host Phanuel

The name Phanuel implies the substance of God. A portion of his obligations incorporate bearing the high position of God, serving truth, and filling in as the holy messenger of judgment. He is likewise a lead celestial host of contrition.

Lead celestial host Zadkiel

Zadkiel is the chief heavenly messenger of opportunity,kindness,and kindheartedness. He is additionally the benefactor holy messenger of every one of those that excuse. In the Bible, perhaps of the main job he played was preventing Abraham from forfeiting Isaac. His effect on people assists with rousing pardoning to permit them to achieve profound opportunity.

Lead celestial host Jegudiel

Jegudiel, otherwise called chief heavenly messenger Jehudiel, is the heavenly messenger of work. His job is to direct those in places of liability. He is their guide and protector and assists them with guaranteeing they work to commend God. In the Catholic framework, Jegudiel is the conveyor of the benevolent love of God. Christians portray Jegudiel holding a crown, which represents his compensation for fruitful otherworldly workers.

Lead celestial host Jophiel

Jophiel Archangel Jophiel is among the scriptural holy messengers' names list known for being the holy messenger of magnificence and astuteness. In spite of the fact that holy messengers don't have a conclusive orientation, Jophiel has a ladylike nature. She functions as a supporter of specialists and imaginative brightening. Jophiel shows the external awareness of Power of Light inside oneself and sends new plans to individuals.

Lead celestial host Haniel

Haniel is in this rundown of names of heavenly messengers and their obligations in the Bible since she is one of the seven lead celestial hosts. Her name implies Joy of God or the Grace of God. She likewise assumes the part of heavenly correspondence and goes about as an immediate section between a human's lower energy and the higher energy conditions of the divine domains.

Lead celestial host Barachiel

Barachiel is a lead celestial host who is a benefactor of family and hitched life. He is the holy messenger doled out by God to look after converts or God's taken on kids and help them in their lives. In the book of Enoch, Barachiel is one of the radiant sovereigns. He has many serving holy messengers that go to him. The Roman Catholic portrays him holding a bread bin which represents the favors of youngsters presented to guardians by God.

Lead celestial host Camael

Camael is a chief heavenly messenger of solidarity, fortitude, and war. Christians accept Camael is the head of the powers that tossed Adam and Eve out of the Garden of Aden. That is likewise the explanation his title is the holy messenger of annihilation. The name Camael implies he who sees God since he had the pleasure of remaining in God's presence.

Lead celestial host Jeremiel

Jeremiel is among the male heavenly messenger names in the Bible, and that implies the leniency of God. His job is to assist people with perceptiveness and prophetic dreams. Jeremiel is likewise a heavenly messenger of feelings and helps individuals to investigate their lives. In the post-Christian world, his obligations advanced to being the guard of paradise and looking after and directing the sacred departed in their the hereafter venture.

CHAPTER FOUR

Does Angels protect us ?

"Without a doubt holy messengers frequently watch us from mishaps and mischief, from enticement and sin. They may appropriately be talked about as divine messengers. Many individuals have borne and may bear declaration to the direction and security that they have gotten from sources past their regular vision. Without the assist that we with getting from the steady presence of the Holy Spirit, and from conceivable blessed heavenly messengers, the challenges of life would be incredibly increased.

"The normal conviction, in any case,that each individual naturally introduced to the world has a divine messenger relegated to be with that individual continually,isn't upheld by accessible proof.A holy messenger might be a heavenly messenger however he come exclusively as relegated to give us unique assistance. As a matter of fact, the steady presence of the Holy Spirit would appear to make such aconsistent, saintly friendship superfluous.

"In this way, until additional information is gotten, we might say that holy messengers might be shipped off monitor us as per our need; yet we can't say with conviction that there is an extraordinary heavenly messenger to accompany each individual.

I would love to share my personal experience, thoughts and emotions how i am very much connected to Angels.

I consider Angels as my friend and all the incidents which I am going to share are true story.

Ever since I learned angel therapy I always feel that angels are around and protecting me.

I want to share a personal experience with you.

"A half year in the wake of learning holy messenger treatment, we got the news that my aunt (tai ji), who lived in Siliguri, had passed away. We used to live in Kolkata. At the point when we got the news it was evening. When we got the news, all of us left for to Siliguri. It was night when we left for Siliguri. The street was extremely hazardous and there was plausible of a mishap. It was raining heavily. Also, the street was dull as well. The thruway street was too hazardous and just truck was going all through the street. We were conscious as far as possible and I was going the entire night recalling Angel. It was still raining even in the first part of the day. In the glass of the vehicle, I saw such a shape made of water that the shape closely resembled a holy messenger was. It very well may be sounding peculiar and you might be feeling that, it could be a mix-up of my eyes, however I accept that in that feared night, the heavenly messengers were with us as far as possible and were safeguarding us".

I got feather from such a place where getting it is unimaginable. Yet, I have it.

On the absolute first day of my therapy, out of nowhere a feather came flying and sat on my chest. Seeing this, everybody got a goosebumps.

Each an everytime I travel Angels protect me all the time.

How our archangels protect us:
Let us first understand
Who are our Archangels:
An archangel is an angel considered to be of the highest rank in popular consciousness, due to John Milton's Paradise Lost, though theological works actually place them as the second lowest amongst nine orders. The word archangel itself is usually associated with the Abrahamic religions, but beings that are very similar to archangels are found in a number of other religious traditions. Archangels also appear in the religious texts of Gnosticism. The four most common archangels are Michael, Gabriel, Raphael, and Uriel.

The English word archangel is derived from Greek word arkhangelos. The word that signifies "first, head, or boss"; and angelos, and that signifies "courier of God." So, lead celestial hosts are the central couriers of God.Chief heavenly messengers are incredibly strong divine creatures. Each has a forte and addresses a part of God. You can consider chief heavenly messengers aspects on the essence of God, a definitive gem and diamond of the universe. These features, or lead celestial hosts, are crystals that transmit Divine light and love in unambiguous ways to everybody on Earth.

The lead celestial hosts are one of God's unique manifestations, and they existed long prior to humanity or coordinated religions. They have a place with God, not to any explicit philosophy. In this manner, lead celestial hosts work with individuals of various convictions furthermore, ways. They work with any individual who asks, truth be told. Fine art depicts chief heavenly messengers c-or swanlike wings, rather than imaginative portrayals of angels as infants with little wings.

Michael and Gabriel are perceived as lead celestial hosts in Judaism, Islam, and by most Christians. A few Protestants believe Michael to be the main lead celestial host. Raphael — referenced in the deuterocanonical Book of Tobit — is likewise perceived as a main holy messenger in the Catholic and Eastern Orthodox chapels. Gabriel, Michael, and Raphael are worshiped in the Roman Catholic Church with a devour September 29 (somewhere in the range of 1921 and 1969, March 24 for Gabriel and October 24 for Raphael), and in the Eastern Orthodox Church on November 8 (in the event that the Julian schedule is utilized, this compares to November 21 in the Gregorian).The named chief heavenly messengers in Islam are Jibrael, Mikael, Israfil, and Azrael. Jewish writing, like the Book of Enoch, additionally specifies Metatron as a chief heavenly messenger, called the "most elevated of the holy messengers", however the acknowledgment of this heavenly messenger isn't standard in that frame of mind of the confidence.

A few parts of the religions referenced have recognized a gathering of seven Archangels, however the named heavenly messengers fluctuate, contingent upon the source. Gabriel, Michael, and Raphael are constantly referenced; different chief heavenly messengers change, yet most generally incorporate Uriel.

In Zoroastrianism, consecrated texts imply the six extraordinary Amesha Spenta (in a real sense "Bounteous/ Holy Immortals") of Ahura Mazda.

A rising number of specialists in human sciences, religious philosophy and reasoning accept that Zoroastrianism contains the earliest refining of ancient faith in angels.

The Amesha Spentas (Avestan: Amesa Spenta, signifying "interminable blessedness") of Zoroastrianism are compared to chief heavenly messengers. They exclusively possess undying bodies that work in the actual world to safeguard, guide, and move humankind and the soul world. The Avesta makes sense of the beginning and nature of lead celestial hosts or Amesha Spentas.

To keep up with harmony, Ahura Mazda participated in the principal demonstration of creation, recognizing his Holy Spirit Spenta Mainyu, the Archangel of honorableness. Ahura Mazda additionally recognized from himself six more Amesha Spentas, who, alongside Spenta Mainyu, supported the production of the actual universe. Then he regulated the improvement of sixteen grounds, each saturated with an interesting social impetus determined to energize the development of particular human populaces. The Amesha Spentas were accused of safeguarding these heavenly terrains and through their radiation, likewise accepted to adjust each separate populace in support of God.

The Amesha Spentas as properties of God are:

Spenta Mainyu (Pahlavi:Spenamino):

lit. "Abundant Spirit"

Asha Vahishta (Phl. Ardwahisht):

lit. "Most noteworthy Truth"

Vohu Mano (Phl. Vohuman):

lit. "Noble Mind"

Khshathra Vairya (Phl. Shahrewar):

lit. "Helpful Dominion"

Spenta Armaiti (Phl. Spandarmad):

lit. "Heavenly Devotion"

Haurvatat (Phl. Hordad):

lit. "Flawlessness or Health"

Ameretat (Phl. Amurdad):
lit. "Everlasting status"
The Hebrew Bible purposes the term (malakhey Elohim; Angels of God) The Hebrew word for holy messenger is "malakh," and that implies courier, for the heavenly messengers " (malakhey Adonai; Angels of the Lord) are God's couriers to perform different missions - for example 'heavenly messenger of death'; (b'nei elohim; children of God) and (ha-q'doshim; the sacred ones) to allude to creatures generally deciphered as celestial couriers. Different terms are utilized in later texts, for example, (ha-elyonim, the upper ones, or the preeminent ones). References to heavenly messengers are phenomenal in Jewish writing besides in later works like the Book of Daniel, however they are referenced momentarily in the tales of Jacob (who as per one understanding grappled with a heavenly messenger) and Lot (who was cautioned by heavenly messengers of the looming obliteration of the urban communities of Sodom and Gomorrah). Daniel is the principal scriptural figure to allude to individual heavenly messengers by name. It is hence generally conjectured that Jewish interest in heavenly messengers created during the Babylonian captivity. According to Rabbi Simeon ben Lakish of Tiberias (230-270 A.D.), explicit names for the holy messengers were brought back by the Jews from Babylon.

There are no unequivocal references to lead celestial hosts in the accepted texts of the Hebrew Bible. In post-Biblical Judaism, certain heavenly messengers came to take on a specific importance and created remarkable characters and jobs. However these lead celestial hosts were accepted to have positioned among the superb host, no methodical progressive system at any point created. Metatron is viewed as one of the greatest of the heavenly messengers in Merkavah and Kabbalist magic and frequently fills in as a copyist. He is momentarily referenced in the Talmud, and figures unmistakably in Merkavah magical texts. Michael, who fills in as a hero and promoter for Israel, is viewed especially affectionately. Gabriel is referenced in the Book of Daniel and momentarily in the Talmud, as well as numerous Merkavah magical texts. The earliest references to lead celestial hosts are in the writing of the intertestamental periods (e.g., 4 Esdras 4:36).

In the Kabbalah there are twelve lead celestial hosts, each relegated to a certain sephira: Metatron, Raziel, Cassiel, Zadkiel, Camael, Michael, Uriel and Haniel, Raphael and Jophiel, Gabriel, and Sandalphon. Section 20 of the Book of Enoch specifies seven sacred heavenly messengers who watch, that frequently are viewed as the seven lead celestial hosts: Michael, Raphael, Gabriel, Uriel, Saraqael, Raguel, and Remiel. The Life of Adam and Eve records the lead celestial hosts also: Michael, Gabriel, Uriel, Raphael and Joel. Middle age Jewish logician Maimonides made a Jewish saintly ordered progression.

In Catholicism, three are referenced by name:

Gabriel

Michael

Raphael

These three are celebrated together ceremonially on September 29. Each previously had his own gala.

The last option of these distinguishes himself in Tobit 12:15(NAB) in this manner: "I'm Raphael, one of the seven holy messengers who stand and serve before the Glory of the Lord."

The Fourth Book of Esdras, which makes reference to the heavenly messenger Uriel (and furthermore the "lead celestial host" Jeremiel), was well known in the West and was regularly cited by Church Fathers, particularly Ambrose, yet was never viewed as a feature of the Catholic scriptural canon.

The Catholic Church gives no authority acknowledgment to the names given in a few fanciful sources, like Raguel, Saraqael and Remiel (in the Book of Enoch) or Izidkiel, Hanael, and Kepharel (in other such sources).

Eastern Orthodox Tradition makes reference to "an enormous number of archangels"; regardless, only seven lead heavenly hosts are loved by name. Uriel is consolidated, and the other three are most often named Selaphiel, Jegudiel, and Barachiel (an eighth, Jeremiel, is at times included as archangel). The Orthodox Church lauds the Synaxis of the Archangel Michael and the Other Bodiless Powers on November 8 of the Eastern Orthodox stately timetable (for those sanctuaries which follow the Julian Calendar, November 8 falls on November 21 of the state of the art Gregorian Calendar). Other feasting experience days of the Archangels recall the Synaxis of the Archangel Gabriel for March 26 (April 8), and the Miracle of the Archangel Michael at Colossae on September 6 (September 19). Likewise, every Monday all during that time is dedicated to the Angels, with exceptional notification being made in the assembly hymns of Michael and Gabriel. In Orthodox iconography, each angel has a symbolic representation

Michael in the Hebrew language implies "Who is like God?" or "Who is comparable to God?" Michael has been depicted from earliest Christian times as, an in his right commandant hand a spear with which he pursues Lucifer/ Satan, and in his left hand a green palm branch. At the most noteworthy place of the spear, there is a material strip with a red cross. The Archangel Michael is especially seen as the Guardian of the Orthodox Faith and a competitor against obscenities.

Gabriel in Hebrews means "God is my fortitude" or "Force of God". He is the emissary of the privileged insights of God, especially the Incarnation of God and any leftover insider facts associated with it. He is depicted as follows: In his right hand, he holds a light with a lit shape inside, and in his left hand, an impression of green jasper. The mirror suggests the knowledge of God as confidential.

Raphael is a jewish name which implies "God recovers" or "God Heals". Raphael is depicted driving Tobit (who is conveying a fish caught in the Tigris) with his right hand and holding a specialist's alabaster compartment in his left hand.

Uriel in the jewish language means "God is my light", or "Light of God" (II Esdras 4:1, 5:20). He is depicted holding a sword in his right hand, and a fire in his left.

Sealtiel implies "Go-between of God". He is depicted with his face and eyes cut down, holding his hands on his chest in request.

Jegudiel connotes "Glorifier of God". He is depicted bearing a splendid wreath in his right hand and a triple-thonged whip in his left hand.

Barachiel means "Leaned toward by God". He is depicted getting a handle on a white rose against his chest.

Jerahmeel means "God's amplification". He is adored as an inspirer and awakener of lifted up thoughts that raise a person toward God (2 Esdras 4:36). As an eighth, he is on occasion included as a lead divine host.

The Ethiopian Orthodox Tewahedo Church loves the four chief heavenly messengers Michael, Gabriel, Raphael, and Uriel, also as:

Phanuel, signifying "Face of God"

Raguel, signifying "Companion of God"

Ramiel or Remiel,signifying "Roar of God"

In the ordinance of the Ethiopian Orthodox Tewahedo Church, 1 Enoch portrays Saraqael as one of the holy messengers who look after "the spirits that transgression in the soul".

In Islam, the referenced archangels (Karubiyin) in the Islamic analytical customs are:

Gabriel (Jibrail or Jibril in Arabic). Gabriel is supposed to be the chief heavenly messenger liable for communicating God's disclosures to all prophets, including uncovering the Quran to Muhammad and initiating him to recount it. Different hadiths (customs) notice his part in conveying messages from "God the Almighty" to the prophets.

Michael (Mikhail or Mikal in Arabic). Michael is many times portrayed as the chief heavenly messenger of kindness who is liable for carrying precipitation and roar to Earth.

Raphael (Israfil or Rafail in Arabic). The name isn't referenced in the Quran. Believed in Islam by some to be the heavenly messenger of the trumpet answerable for flagging the approaching of Judgment Day.

Azrael (Azrail in Arabic, additionally called Malak al-Maut, in a real sense "heavenly messenger of death"). Taking the spirit of the dead to paradise or damnation. The name isn't referenced in the Quran.

In the Gnostic codex On the Origin of the World, the age named Sophia sends seven lead divine hosts from her light to save the Archon Sabaoth, the offspring of Yaldabaoth, after the experts of Chaos make fight in the Seven Heavens. He is then situated in a brilliant domain over the twelve heavenly powers of Chaos and transforms into the accomplice of Zoe (the beginning phase Eve), who gives him data on the eighth heaven, while the seven lead heavenly hosts stand before them. In The Sophia of Jesus Christ and Eugnostos the Blessed, the beginning phase Adam makes crowds of heavenly creatures and boss angels without number.

Various traditions

Adjust

Mediums from time to time accomplice boss angels in Kabbalistic style with various seasons or parts, or even tones. In some Kabbalah-based systems of formal witchcraft, all of the four of the essential boss angels (Gabriel, Michael, Raphael and Uriel) are gathered as safeguarding the four quarters, or course, and their relating tones are connected with puzzling properties.Lucifer or Satan in Christian practices, or Iblis in Islam, is seen as a lead divine host by Satanists and various non-Satanists, but most non-Satanists consider him despicable and tumbled from God's.

CHAPTER FIVE

Seven Archangels

The idea of Seven Archangels is tracked down in certain works of early Jewish writing. In those texts, they are referred to as the holy messengers who serve God straightforwardly.

Book of scriptures

The term lead celestial host itself isn't tracked down in the Hebrew Bible or the Christian Old Testament, and in the Greek New Testament the term chief heavenly messenger just happens in 1 Thessalonians 4:16 and the Epistle of Jude 1:9, where it is utilized of Michael, who in Daniel 10:12 is called 'one of the main rulers,' and 'the extraordinary sovereign'. In the Septuagint this is delivered "the extraordinary angel."

The possibility of seven chief heavenly messengers is most expressly expressed in the deuterocanonical Book of Tobit when Raphael uncovers himself, proclaiming: "I'm Raphael, one of the seven heavenly messengers who stand in the radiant presence of the Lord, prepared to serve him." (Tobit 12,15) The other two holy messengers referenced by name in the Bible are lead celestial host Michael and heavenly messenger Gabriel. The four names of different chief heavenly messengers come from custom.

1 Enoch

One such custom of chief heavenly messengers comes from the Old Testament scriptural unauthenticated written work, the third century BCE Book of the Watchers, known as 1 Enoch or the Book of Enoch, at last converged into the Enochic Pentateuch. This account is subsidiary with the Book of Giants, which likewise references the incredible archangels[5][6] and was made piece of the Ethiopian Orthodox Tewahedo Church's scriptural standard. Albeit predominant in Jewish and early Christian missional customs and the early Christian Fathers, the Book of Enoch slowly tumbled from scholarly and strict status, and by the seventh century was dismissed from the sanctioned sacred writings of any remaining Christian categories, a restricted and obscure work. The different enduring oral practices related many varying arrangements of archangels.

The names entered Jewish practice during the Babylonian bondage (605 BCE). Babylonian old stories and cosmology, an early Mesopotamian convictions under the dualistic impact of Zoroastrianism, based on human and zoomorphic portrayals of stars, planets, and heavenly bodies, including the four children of the Sky Father conveying the Winged Sun, the lofty position of Wisdom. First the prophet Daniel, then, at that point, creators, for example, Ezekiel hebraized this folklore, likening the Babylonian groups of stars with dynamic structures held to be "children of the divine beings", holy messengers of the Lord of Israel, and great creature cherubim. The 2 BC Book of the Parables names the four heavenly messengers going with the Ancient of Days, remaining before the Lord of Spirits, "the voices of those upon the four sides amplifying the Lord of Glory": Michael, Raphael, Gabriel, and Phanuel.

The Book of the Watchers records the heavenly messengers who in antediluvian times mediated for humankind against the rebel spirits named "the Watchers": Michael, Gabriel, Raphael, and Uriel.

The earliest unambiguous Christian references are in the late fifth to mid sixth 100 years: Pseudo-Dionysius gives them as Michael, Gabriel, Raphael, Uriel, Camael, Jophiel, and Zadkiel. In most Protestant Christian oral practices just Michael and Gabriel are alluded to as "chief heavenly messengers", which repeats the most standard Muslim view, while Roman-Rite Catholic Christian customs likewise incorporate Raphael to finish a gathering of three. Through its Byzantine practice, notwithstanding, the Catholic Church perceives seven lead celestial hosts out and out, in some cases named, once in a while anonymous other than the three referenced previously.

Arrangements of characters alluded to as "holy messengers" likewise exist in more modest strict customs generally viewed as medium or odd. A reference to seven chief heavenly messengers showed up in an eighth or ninth century charm credited to Auriolus, a "worker of God" in north-western Spain. He gives a request to "all you patriarchs Michael, Gabriel, Cecitiel, Uriel, Raphael, Ananiel, Marmoniel.

In the Catholic Church, three lead celestial hosts are referenced by name in its standard of sacred text: Michael, Gabriel, and Raphael. Raphael shows up in the deuterocanonical Book of Tobit, where he is depicted as "one of the seven holy messengers who stand prepared and enter before the brilliance of the master of spirits", an expression reviewed in Revelation 8:2-6.

Some Eastern Orthodox Churches, exemplified in the Orthodox Slavonic Bible (Ostrog Bible, Elizabeth Bible, and later thus Russian Synodal Bible), perceive as definitive likewise 2 Esdras, which specifies Uriel.

The Eastern Orthodox Church and Eastern Catholic Churches of the Byzantine custom worship seven lead celestial hosts and in some cases an eighth. Michael, Gabriel, Raphael, Uriel, Selaphiel (Salathiel), Jegudiel (Jehudiel), Barachiel, and the eighth, Jerahmeel (Jeremiel) (The Synaxis of the Chief of the Heavenly Hosts, Archangel Michael and the Other Heavenly Bodiless Powers: Feast Day: November 8).The Melkite Catholic Church also worships the Archangel Raguel.

As well as Uriel, the Book of Enoch, not viewed as sanctioned by any of these Christian places of worship, makes reference to (part 20) Raguel, Saraqâêl, and Remiel, while other fanciful sources give rather the names Izidkiel, Hanael, and Kepharel.

In the Ethiopian Orthodox practice the seven Archangels are named as Michael, Gabriel, Raphael, Uriel, Raguel, Phanuel, and Sachiel. In the Coptic Orthodox practice the seven chief heavenly messengers are named as Michael, Gabriel, Raphael, Suriel, Zadkiel, Sarathiel, and Ananiel.

In Anglican and Episcopal practice, there are three or four chief heavenly messengers in the schedule for September 29, the dining experience of St Michael and All Angels (likewise called Michaelmas), to be specific Michael, Gabriel, and Raphael, and frequently additionally Uriel.

Different customs

Alter

Albeit in the Book of Enoch, Ramiel is depicted as one of the heads of the 200 Grigori, the fallen holy messengers, the pioneer is recognized as Semjaza. Different names got from pseudepigrapha and perceived by Eastern Orthodox and Oriental Orthodox places of worship are Selaphiel,

Jegudiel, and Raguel.

In Ismailism, there are seven cherubim, similar to the Seven Archangels requested to kneel before Qadar, of whom Iblis refuses.

In Yazidism, there are seven lead celestial hosts, named Jabra'il, Mika'il, Rafa'il (Israfil), Dadra'il, Azrail and Shamkil (Shemna'il) and Azazil, who are spreads from God endowed with care of the creation.

Seven holy messengers or lead celestial hosts compare to days of the week: Michael (Sunday), Gabriel (Monday), Uriel (Tuesday), Raphael (Wednesday), Selaphiel (Thursday), Raguel or Jegudiel (Friday), and Barachiel (Saturday).[citation needed]

Different mysterious frameworks partner every chief heavenly messenger with one of the conventional "seven illuminating presences" (old style planets apparent to the unaided eye): the Sun, the Moon, Mercury, Venus, Mars, Jupiter, and Saturn; yet there is conflict concerning which lead celestial host compares to which body.

As indicated by Rudolf Steiner, four chief heavenly messengers administer the seasons: spring is Raphael, summer is Uriel, fall is Michael, and winter is Gabriel.

In the early Gnostic message On the Origin of the World, the age named Sophia sends seven lead celestial hosts to safeguard the Archon Sabaoth and carry him to the eighth heaven.

Albeit all chief heavenly messengers offer direction, intelligence, and motivation, each lead celestial host assumes a particular part and capability.

This implies you must be know about the chief heavenly messengers to know which lead celestial host to contact.

The following are seven lead celestial hosts that are more than once referred to in profound texts.

Here are the implications of name of the seven lead celestial hosts:

Michael: He who is as God

Raphael: God recuperates

Gabriel: God is my solidarity

Jophiel: Beauty of God

Ariel: Lion of God

Azrael: Whom God makes a difference

Chamuel: He who sees God

CHAPTER SIX

Michael

Lead celestial host Michael is God's top holy messenger, driving each of the holy messengers in paradise. He is otherwise called Saint Michael. Michael signifies "Who is like God?" Other spellings of Michael's name incorporate Mikhael, Mikael, Mikail, and Mikhail.

Michael's fundamental attributes are uncommon strength and fortitude. Michael battles for good to beat malevolence and enables adherents to set their confidence in God ablaze with energy. He safeguards and protects individuals who love God.Individuals in some cases request Michael's assistance to acquire the fortitude they need to defeat their feelings of dread, get solidarity to oppose compulsions to sin and on second thought make the wisest decision and remain protected in risky circumstances.

Images of Archangel Michael

Michael is in many cases portrayed in craftsmanship using a sword or a lance, addressing his job as the celestial forerunner in otherworldly fights. Other fight images that address Michael incorporate defensive layer and standards. Michael's other fundamental job as a critical heavenly messenger of death is represented in workmanship that portrays him gauging individuals' spirits on scales.

Energy Color

Blue is the holy messenger light beam related with Archangel Michael. It represents power, assurance, confidence, boldness, and strength

Job in Religious Texts

Michael holds the differentiation of being highlighted more frequently than some other named heavenly messenger in significant strict texts. The Torah, Bible, and Qur'an all notice Michael.

In the Torah, God picks Michael to safeguard and shield Israel as a country. Daniel 12:21 of the Torah depicts Michael as "the incredible sovereign" who will safeguard God's kin in any event, during the battle among great and evil toward the apocalypse. In the Zohar (an essential book in the Jewish mystery called Kabbalah), Michael accompanies the spirits of noble individuals to paradise.

The Bible portrays Michael in Revelation 12:7-12 driving multitudes of heavenly messengers that fight Satan and his evil spirits during the world's last clash. The Bible says Michael and celestial soldiers at long last arise successful, which likewise makes reference to in 1 Thessalonians 4:16 that Michael will go with Jesus Christ when he gets back to Earth.

The Qur'an cautions in Al-Baqara 2:98: "Whoever is a foe to God and his holy messengers and his missionaries, to Gabriel and Michael - - lo! God is a foe to the individuals who reject the confidence." Muslims accept that God has allocated Michael to compensate exemplary individuals for the great they do during their natural lifetimes.

Other Religious Roles

Many individuals accept that Michael works with divine messengers to speak with kicking the bucket individuals about confidence and to accompany the spirits of devotees to paradise after they pass on.

The Catholic, Orthodox, Anglican, and Lutheran houses of worship venerate Michael as Saint Michael. He fills in as the supporter holy person of individuals who work in perilous circumstances, for example, military staff, police and security officials, and paramedics. As a holy person, Michael fills in as a model of valor and strikingly working for equity.

The Seventh-Day Adventist and Jehovah's Witness places of worship say that Jesus Christ was Michael before Christ came to Earth. The Church of Jesus Christ of Latter-day Saints says that Michael is presently the wonderful type of Adam, the main made human.

Chief heavenly messenger Michael is one of the most worshiped heavenly messengers in the Christian confidence. It's conceivable you've perused or known about him previously. You might have no clue about what his identity is.

I'm here to help you to look further into Archangel Michael and how you can best associate with him, independent of what your current degree of knowledge and comprehension of him is. Lead celestial host Michael is one of numerous heavenly messengers that are continuously watching out for us.

Here is a captivating being from the brilliant domains that merits our consideration.

Significance of Name: He who is as God

Job: Archangel Michael is the most notable and most impressive lead celestial host. Michael's job is to carry security to us. He is a fighter that is lined up with fortitude, strength, and equity.

In snapshots of emergency, Michael is the lead celestial host you ought to call upon. He will offer direction and heavenly security to the people who need him at the most lucky time.

Lead celestial host Michael most frequently uncovers himself as a flash of blue light. Utilize blue as an update that you are being safeguarded by Archangel Michael

Michael is depicted as a holy messenger of consideration in the sacred texts of the Bible, the Qur'an, and the Torah.

As well as being an "lead celestial host," Michael is a very rare example of heavenly messengers who have this most noteworthy title. Despite the fact that the expression "lead celestial host" could allude to quite a few holy messengers, the Bible just notices Michael as a vital courier.

In truth, the Bible depicts Michael the Archangel as a head of heavenly messengers.

As a pioneer, fighter, and hero of boldness and conventionality, Michael is a good example for us all. He is notable for his job as a gatekeeper of both the land and its occupants. In his job as administrator of heavenly messengers, Michael views his obligations exceptionally in a serious way.

Truth be told, it has been anticipated that Michael the Archangel will have a huge impact toward the apocalypse. Regardless of the Bible's idea that he will assume a part, it is obscure how.

Thus, there is no question that Michael will show up for anybody who has confidence in him!

Images of Archangel Michael

Pictures and images related with Archangel Michael are not notable, however there are a significant number of them. The craftsmanship portrays him as a gallant champion of God as well as a safeguard of individuals.

Authority level weaponry is continually available to him. A portion of these incorporate the fire bladed sword and the safeguard. This holy messenger of fast and intense equity is likewise regularly envisioned using a bunch of scales. His wingspan is noteworthy, and he radiates a feeling that all is well with the world in his disposition.

Emblematic of solidarity, backbone, and insurance, blue is associated with Michael the Archangel. Regardless of whether you mean to speak with him, it's a pleasant variety to have at the top of the priority list as an indication of his energy and soul.

Messages of Archangel Michael

Lead celestial host Michael speaks with people in different ways, once in a while straightforwardly and some of the time through designation to different heavenly messengers. All things considered, he is a commandant.

We ought to expect a ton from this head of heavenly messengers with regards to our prosperity and what's to come.

Already, he has given us the message that he will help us in the midst of huge catastrophes, like the apocalypse. This message is pertinent on a worldwide and individual level. On the off chance that you're carrying on with a difficult situation throughout everyday life, he could have a remark to you.

Messages of truth and equity are constantly conveyed by the Archangel Michael, as these are values he holds dear. Because of his different obligations, he will frequently convey his messages with a harsh tone and a fast speed.

With regards to correspondence, individuals remember him for his legitimate manner of speaking and his capacity to cause them to feel appreciated.

For the individuals who stress assuming they're receiving Michael's messages, they might anticipate that he should stand up and be obtuse! Regardless of his sort disposition, the Angel likes to be heard obviously the initial time around.

Regardless of whether you ask Archangel Michael for help, he is typically the one to approach. Luckily, he's not the sort to become involved with all the imagery.

Messages from Archangel Michael are not difficult to perceive and ought to leave you with a couple of inquiries!

What is Michael the lead celestial host power?

Lead celestial hosts Michael is undying, with godlike strength, speed, resistance, a sonic cry, the capacity to fly, destructive blood, special insight, and the ability to speak with creatures.

Who does chief heavenly messenger Michael secure?

Michael is an unquestionably strong holy messenger who monitors and safeguards the individuals who revere God. He is profoundly energetic about equity and truth. Devotees guarantee that when Michael helps and guides people, he talks strongly with them.

What did Archangel Michael resemble?

Long ears, horns, and completely open, frantically moving eyes, as well as his tongue, that hangs out of his lips, damage his face. The holy messenger moves effortlessly, and his wings and covering provide him with the presence of an old legend.

Is Saint Michael a heavenly messenger?

Holy person Michael is a lead celestial host who battles for the positive qualities in the otherworldly domain. He is venerated as a protector of equity, a rescuer of the wiped out, as well as the Church's watchman.

Who is the head of the chief heavenly messengers?

All lead celestial host Michael is God's most impressive heavenly messenger, ordering paradise's holy messengers. Michael is the Leader of the chief heavenly messengers. Michael's name can likewise be spelt as Mikhael, Mikael,

Mikail, and Mikhail.

What is the Archangel Michael's weapon?

Michael's Sword is a monstrous and incredibly strong edge used by the chief heavenly messenger Michael. God by and by gave Michael the sword for him to battle his sibling Lucifer and his defiant army of holy messengers.

Direction from Archangel Michael

Might it be said that you are searching for the assistance of Archangel Michael in your life? How might he best assistance you? Known for diving into fight valiantly, Michael is an astounding watchman. Do you have your own devils to fight with?

At the point when you're at your most reduced, approaching Michael the Archangel for self-guidance is prudent. In the event that you at any point wind up needing support, he's there to loan some assistance. Assuming you're needing backing or consolation, Michael is reasonable previously tuning in.

On all of your own excursions, Archangel Michael can help. Is it true or not that you are uncertain of what your life's central goal is?

In the event that you ask Michael for help, be prepared for a perhaps dull reaction.

We have numerous celestial team promoters here, yet Michael is more disposed to use real love than assuaging with regards to helping other people succeed. In any case, he is the best individual to request help since he sees precisely the amount you could bear.

Step by step instructions to Recognize Archangel Michael

Lead celestial host Michael might have proactively reached you. Signs and signs of this eminent being can be perceived in different ways.

You've Received Messages in a Clear Voice

Lead celestial host Michael sends you obvious indicators and messages without skirting the real issue. You might have heard a voice letting you know something, yet did you hear it plainly? This could be Michael's approach to connecting with everybody in the most straightforward manner conceivable: by utilizing his voice.

He may not be all around as vocal as he used to be constantly or he may simply shout out at specific times. His message, then again, ought to be perfectly clear, and he ought to keep things quick and painless.

In the event that you believe he's attempting to certainly stand out enough to be noticed, you should attempt contemplation or another type of mental purifying.

Glimmers of Blue Radiance Appear

Michael's energy and presence are encapsulated in blue, a mitigating and quieting shade that ought not be disregarded. Look out for blue light or eruptions of blue light that aren't commonly present, as this could be a sign from Michael.

Lead celestial host Michael, in contrast to different heavenly messengers, doesn't believe you should miss his fragile messages. In the event that you at any point see the blue light and believe it's coming from Michael, he should make it exceptionally obvious. As he's putting it, he is here to help you!

Unexpectedly You Start Feeling Warm or Tingly

Since our faculties are interlaced with our interesting instinct, our divine messengers much of the time speak with us through them.

Michael might be attempting to speak with you by causing you to feel warm or shivery at very badly designed times. In the event that you see this occurrence, it very well might be smart to ask or think.

Your Dreams have been Calm and Clear

After his contentions, Archangel Michael offers tranquility to you, and his essential objective is to shield you. This could be a message from the chief heavenly messenger himself in the event that you've encountered clear and consoling dreams, particularly ones in which you saw heavenly messengers.

Holy messengers ordinarily speak with us through the psyche mind, very much like our faculties.

Really unusual (consider teeth emerging or winds), Michael will visit with an unmistakable message and point.

At the point when you get up, you ought to be helped to remember it, and reflecting or supplicating as a coherent subsequent stage in your everyday custom ought to be essential for your daily schedule too.

It's generally smart to let Michael know that you heard him plainly!

You Have much More Michaels in Your Life

The most effective ways to connect with somebody are frequently the least complex. The quantity of Michaels in your day to day existence is by all accounts expanding at a disturbing rate.

Notwithstanding his gruffness, Archangel Michael is eminent for his comical inclination, and he might continue to send you Michaels until you look for him!

Lead celestial host Michael Number

Lead celestial host Michael seems, by all accounts, to be the most firmly related with number 11 among our heavenly messengers. The heavenly messenger number 11 might be a way for him to reach you, yet what's the significance here? What is it about Michael the Archangel that makes the number 1 so noticeable?

Instinct, the spirit, and boldness are emphatically connected with holy messenger number 1. Perhaps of our most grounded holy messenger, Archangel Michael never wonders whether or not to take the side of the powerless and defenseless. It is notable that the number 11 is connected with otherworldliness and upgraded instinct.

Everything really revolves around believing your own singular instinct, which is addressed by the number 1, and everything revolves around confiding in your very own senses to help other people. Our essential gatekeeper and profound aide, Archangel Michael, is best addressed by the number 11.

Michael might be attempting to definitely stand out enough to be noticed in the event that you continue to see the number 111. Notwithstanding the few different signs recorded, this figure ought not be ignored.

Lead celestial host Michael will inform you as to whether he's looking to interface, as you've previously found. He may likewise associate with you through holy messenger number 1111 or heavenly messenger number 11111.

Instructions to Connect with Archangel Michael

Imploring can be a basic strategy to speak with Archangel Michael. You can be puzzled regarding where to start or what to say. Evaluate these elective approaches to interfacing as well as dealing with your request abilities by appealing to yourself.

Set up an Altar

Building a special raised area in your home can be useful in different otherworldly settings. Lead celestial host Michael's sanctuary is an incredible asset for interfacing with him.

Consider what contributions you can make to him, as well as any going with signs or images, and make plans to incorporate these in your special raised area.

While thinking or loving at the special raised area, it's consistently really smart to light a flame in blue or perhaps a St. Michael flame. To associate with your heavenly messengers, zeroing in on the altar is significant.

Supplicate on Sunday or Michael's Day

Sundays which are otherwise called Michael's day is the ideal day to offer supplications to Archangel Michael. You might find it more straightforward to speak with him on the off chance that you implore him on Sundays.

A great many people use Sundays as a day to loosen up and consider their lives. To assist you with both of these undertakings, Michael is accessible!

Utilize the Blue Color

As may be obvious, blue has forever been Michael the Archangel's number one tone. Adding blue tone to your way of life will just assist you with bettering use Archangel Michael's dynamism and strength.

Utilize blue in your home, your closet, your special raised area, and your everyday daily practice. On the off chance that anything grabs Michael's attention, he'll observe!

Chief heavenly messenger Michael Prayers

Is it safe to say that you are uncertain about the proper method for tending to Archangel Michael? Despite the fact that there is certainly not a set in stone technique to speak with your heavenly messengers and supplicate, here are a few ideas for petitions that you could utilize while conversing with Michael!

Petition for Courage and Bravery

On the off chance that you struggling with managing what is going on? Michael is accessible to help and support you as you face your difficulties. In the midst of dread, go to Archangel Michael.

Please, St. Michael, give me your extraordinary boldness with the goal that I can take on this test. During this snapshot of fear I depend on your boldness and skill, and I thank you for not being terrified, so be it.

Supplication for Spiritual Clarity

Every single one of our holy messengers can furnish us with signs or explanation here and there. On the off chance that you're in a situation where you don't have the foggiest idea what to do, Michael can help.

Much obliged to you, St. Michael, for directing me on the correct way. I'm confused on what to do given the conditions I wind up in the present moment. Kindly acknowledge my genuine appreciation for your help and sagacious guidance.

Supplication for Crisis

Chief heavenly messenger Michael is notable for coming to the guide of individuals in need when the world is by all accounts self-destructing. In the domain of battle, he is an exceptional figure. Notwithstanding what you might think, Michael is a lot of a heavenly messenger who guides us through our own fights.

As a request to St. Michael, kindly permit me to explore this difficult second in my life safely. Kindly aide and relieve me as I look for direction and solace. I want you like never before this moment. Much obliged to you for continually watching out for me, Lord.

Supplication for Reassurance

Previously, have you settled on a significant choice and been befuddled assuming that it was the right one? With regards to directing individuals in the correct heading and making a move, Archangel Michael has everything.

Dear St. Michael, I ask your absolution. Is this the best game-plan for me? For equity and goodness, I ask that you lead me in the correct bearing. It's been a joy working with you.

We are under the insurance of Archangel Michael, a powerful heavenly messenger who is continuously paying special attention to us. In the midst of affliction, you might depend on his solace and shrewdness.

Have you at any point had a feeling of Michael's presence around you? Kindly offer your encounters in the remarks area!

Lead celestial host Metatron alongside Archangel Gabriel are two other strong heavenly messengers who can help you on your way to edification.

CHAPTER SEVEN

Raphael

Lead celestial host Raphael is known as the heavenly messenger of mending. He attempts to recuperate individuals' brains, spirits, and bodies so they can appreciate harmony and great wellbeing to the furthest reaches of God's will for them.At the point when Raphael is near, you might encounter various indications of his merciful consideration for you. Here are a few indications of Raphael's presence when he is close by:Raphael Brings New Information or Ideas that Promote Healing Raphael frequently infers new data or novel thoughts that you can use as important apparatuses to seek after mending from whatever is ailing you, adherents say.In their book, "The Complete Idiot's Guide to Connecting With Your Angels," Cecily Channer and Damon Brown express: "Besides in circumstances where an individual's passing or disease is essential for their general heavenly arrangement, Archangel Raphael will vivaciously advance mending. Search for him to motivate you with abrupt experiences giving you the perfect data to help the recuperating."

"Lead celestial host Raphael much of the time answers petitions to God by murmuring ideas that you hear as considerations, sentiments, dreams, and dreams," composes Doreen Virtue in her book, "The Healing

Miracles of Archangel Raphael." When you get serious areas of strength for a to make a positive move, realize that this is an addressed supplication. Follow your hunches and they'll lead you to recharged harmony."

Mary LaSota and Harriet Sternberg write in their book: "Lead celestial host Raphael: Loving Messages of Joy, Love, and Healing for Us as well as Our Earth," "Raphael is known to give petitions quickly and he will direct you through the mending system. In the event that the mending is for you, watch for some sign: an idea, thought, or internal message. On the off chance that there is a fundamental justification behind the ailment, like contempt, for instance, Raphael will here and there bring up this to you. It might then be changed to cherish, along these lines accelerating your recuperation time."

Not exclusively will Raphael assist you with sorting out how best to seek after mending for yourself, yet he will likewise direct clinical experts to come to the right conclusions about your consideration or the consideration of a friend or family member you're supporting in supplication, compose LaSota and Sternberg in, "Lead celestial host Raphael: Loving Messages of Joy, Love, and Healing for Us as well as Our Earth" "Raphael feels inclined toward those in generally recuperating callings and will here and there direct those people who are uncertain about what bearings to take for fitting medical care for their patients. He will give suggestions for quick mending and aid a clinical emergency by getting together the ideal group of experts to cooperate."

Raphael has a funny bone that individuals frequently notice when he speaks with them about mending bits of knowledge, composes Virtue in, "The Healing Miracles of Archangel Raphael," "Raphael likewise shows a splendid comical inclination in his showcases of help. A model that generally carries a grin to my face is his propensity for pushing books off racks. Many individuals report finding mending books in their homes that they never purchased, or finding ones in their shopping baskets that they didn't put there."

A Fresh Appreciation of Nature

Whenever you notice the magnificence of God's normal creation around you and sense a desire to take great consideration of it, Raphael might be close by, say adherents. Raphael is energetic about persuading individuals to seek after mending for themselves as well as for the Earth's current circumstance.

Richard Webster writes in his book, "Raphael: Communicating With the Archangel For Healing and Creativity," "At whatever point you see anything especially lovely or striking in nature, you can say thanks to Raphael for taking care of the planet. Let him know that you will do your part to make the world a superior spot for the current occupants, and furthermore for people in the future. You could decide to do this by getting a portion of the waste abandoned by past guests, or by cleaning up an area that has been upset. You will feel Raphael's presence around you as you do this, and you will likewise feel better about accomplishing something good for the climate."

Help Healing Broken Relationships

One more indication of Raphael's presence with you is direction that you get about how to mend and reestablish connections you have with others that have ended up being broken, devotees say.

"Raphael mends fractures in connections and mental and intense subject matters as well as actual medical affliction," composes Christine Astell in her book, "Gifts from Angels." "An ever increasing number of we are arousing to the comprehension of how firmly connected intense subject matters are to sickness in the body, and that chipping away at the otherworldly levels will assist with a wide range of disease."

The way that Raphael frequently decides to assist with recuperating your connections is by empowering you to convey your sentiments completely to others, compose Linda and Peter Miller-Russo in their book, "Dreaming With the Archangels: A Spiritual Guide to Dream Journeying." "Raphael will assist you with moving from suppression of your sentiments without limit, legitimate, and complete articulation of your responses to life. Until you permit yourself to loosen up your restraints, you will not be able to interface with your more profound inclination nature. Raphael will help you with this by tenderly poking you to communicate your actual sentiments to yourself and everyone around you. This will build the degree of correspondence inside your connections, carrying you nearer to those you love, to God, and to yourself."

Green Light

You might see a go-ahead in the air around you when Raphael is visiting you, say devotees, since his energy compares to the green electromagnetic recurrence on the heavenly messenger light beams.

"He encompasses and sustains individuals with the emerald green light of recuperating," compose Cecily Channer and Damon Brown in "The Complete Idiot's Guide to Connecting With Your Angels."

In "The Healing Miracles of Archangel Raphael," Virtue composes that Raphael is anxious to give you indications of his presence, so you might see his atmosphere's light obviously subsequent to approaching him: "Whenever you call upon Raphael, he's there. The recuperating chief heavenly messenger isn't bashful or unobtrusive in declaring his presence. He believes you should know that he's with you, as an approach to soothing you and lightening pressure along your way to a sound recuperation. ... He sparkles so brilliantly that individuals can see blazes or shines of his emerald green light with their actual eyes."

Chief heavenly messenger Michael and Archangel Raphael cooperate to mend actual agony that outcomes from close to home apprehension. Since your body, brain, and soul are complicatedly associated and cooperate as a framework, any trepidation you experience brings about pressure to your framework that can ultimately appear as actual disease or injury. At the point when that occurs, you can ask both of these incredible holy messengers to unite to help you. This is the way to work with Michael and Raphael as accomplices for recuperating: : Look for Courage from Michael and Guidance from Raphael

Begin by looking for help from Michael and Raphael that mirrors every one of their claims to fame.

Michael is a specialist in enabling individuals with boldness, so you can implore or reflect to associate with Michael and get the fortitude you really want to conquer your trepidation.

Raphael is an expert doctor who recommends the perfect treatment plan for individuals in torment. So you can contact Raphael through petition or contemplation for direction about precisely which moves toward take in your recuperating cycle.

"Chief heavenly messengers Michael and Raphael function admirably pair that their relationship feels much the same as to a kinship. They really complete one another gifts, and together proposition a relentless mix of strong recuperating abililties," composes Doreen Virtue in her book The Miracles of Archangel Michael. "... Despite the fact that Raphael is the head recuperating heavenly messenger, it's dependably useful to request that Michael be engaged with the essence of any alarming circumstance."

Distinguish What Type of Fear is Contributing to Your Pain

Cooperating, Michael and Raphael can check your body to analyze precisely exact thing sort of energy is going through the numerous associations it has with your spirit. Any regrettable energy from dread might be adding to the aggravation you feel.

Request that Michael show you explicitly what sort of dread is a figure causing the actual aggravation you're feeling. For instance, on the off chance that you're experiencing torment in your jaw, it could be from grating your teeth around evening time during bad dreams, and Archangel Michael can liberate you from unfortunate bad dreams.

"Numerous sicknesses have a profound reason," composes Richard Webster in his book Communicating with the Archangel Raphael for Healing and Creativity. "... Issues of this sort can be settled by requesting that Raphael assist you with grasping the fundamental purposes for the sickness. When the first reason is known, you can do whatever it may take to determine the trouble."

Since it's so distressing to be experiencing torment, the trepidation you feel may essentially be an immediate consequence of managing the actual aggravation. All things considered, Michael can give you the harmony you want for going through the recuperating system as Raphael leads you from one stage to another.

"Michael and Raphael cooperate to help us in our recuperating processes; it's anything but an either/or circumstance when holy messengers are involved," composes Eileen Elias Freeman in her book Angelic Healing: Working with Your Angels to Heal Your Life. "At the point when the requirement for mending is serious, as, for instance when somebody is genuinely upset following the passing of a friend or family member, the insurance of Michael is a critical piece of the recuperating system. The extraordinary chief heavenly messenger can, from a figurative perspective, spread his wings around us to protect us from hurtful impacts that could keep us from focusing on our mending."

Michael and Raphael can provide you with a precise conclusion of what's happening in both your body and soul so you can concentrate your mending endeavors in the correct manner.

Relinquish Fear to Clear the Way for Healing

The subsequent stage is essentially to relinquish the apprehension - - and whatever other gloomy feeling that outcomes from dread, like displeasure or tension - - so you can get the mending that Michael and Raphael need to send your direction.

When you utilize your natural freedom of thought decide to relinquish dread, Michael and Raphael can clean up the trepidation that has appended to your body as regrettable energy. "The chief heavenly messengers Michael and Raphael frequently fill in collectively to eliminate pessimistic creatures from individuals and spots," composes Eva-Maria Mora in her book Quantum Angel Healing: Energy Therapy and Communication with Angels.

Mora recommends in Quantum Angel Healing to request that Michael, "If it's not too much trouble, accompany your sword of light and cut all pessimistic enthusiastic associations with people, circumstances, places, and articles that are destructive for myself or potentially deny me of my life force energy" while likewise requesting that Raphael assist with sending his recuperating energy into the circumstance.

"I've seen individuals right away recuperate from persistent agony following Michael's mediation," Virtue writes in The Miracles of Archangel Michael. "That is on the grounds that a great deal of spinal and solid torment originates from dread based lines and negative energy. When Michael eliminates these sources, it disappears."

Raphael is likewise capably viable at letting torment in all free from its structures. "Raphael, as the lead celestial host of mending, needs you to appreciate great wellbeing intellectually, inwardly, profoundly, and genuinely," Webster sends in Communicating with the Archangel Raphael for Healing and Creativity.

CHAPTER EIGHT

Gabriel

This is the Archangel generally considered both Male and Female because of the jobs this Archangel has and the actual appearance frequently given as delicate highlights, tenderness and ladylike attributes in current age. I will allude to the manly side anyway I in all actuality do see the two sides of this delightful Angel when he shows up and gives his messages. Gabriel is otherwise called the Christmas Angel because of giving the message of Christs birth and it led to recognizing him as a courier of God.

In established truth his name 'Areas of strength for signifies God' or 'God is my Strength'. Showing his significance as a communicator and strong associations with the heavenly inside us. Proposing to get us confidence and strength our association with the heavenly maker, God or the One.

Images of Archangel Gabriel...

He is frequently seen with harmony lilies, trumpet, harp or parchments. He has numerous melodic associations and pictures because of this being a method of correspondence and music inspiring feelings, sentiments and recollections. Gabriel utilizes music to pass on messages from soul, when we think to associate with our otherworldly self and through dreams to offer guidance.The harmony lilies are an indication of harmony being proposed to you, in an approach to saying all will be well. In conclusion scrolls offer higher insight and information inside. He comes to give you data applicable to your future yet in addition with the goal that you might figure out your past, your motivation and job in this lifetime.

Jobs of Archangel Gabriel...

This astonishing Archangel is a channel, a communicator and courier of the greatest request. Gabriel will attempt to send your requests to Heaven and soul friends and family, as well as handing-off messages back to you. He works with harmony, persistence and quiet to guarantee that correspondence is clear and exact. Gabriel likewise works with using time productively and permitting additional opportunity to finish significant jobs. In the event that you are running really low on time for a cutoff time and need a little assist with approaching Gabriel to help.

Ultimately he was given the job of looking after youngsters from new children to teens! From their most memorable cry a child conveys an inclination and need, Gabriel sets to work. To guarantee they foster their abilities and to help guardians and gatekeepers to grasp their degree of correspondence. Lead celestial host Gabriel chips away at many levels here so we can become cognizant otherworldly being associated with energy correspondence. This is more profound and more instinctive than our actual voice. Being God's solidarity implies that he can ingrain inside us the 'Never surrender' outlook and tell us the best way to request help when we want it!

Abilities of Archangel Gabriel...

Diverting Divine Messages from the Universe to and through us

Tolerating, Understanding and Relaying Prayers to God.Causing quiet inside upsetting circumstances.

Helping scholars, writers, organizers and strategists...anyone who has an inventive style to compose or draw whether for work or side interest

Looking after youngsters and children so they foster relational abilities and capacities to communicate their thoughts

Impart natural sentiments and cognizant realizing that interfaces all of us on a lively level.Invigorating us continue to go regardless of whether we feel drained and fatigued

Variety Associated with Archangel Gabriel...

There are two fundamental tones, one being white and the second shades of yellow through to gold. White brings lucidity, clear correspondence and understanding. While the golds have higher data, inspiring profound energy and rising. Both are elevating with Gabriels energy being a lot of about raising vibrations and starting comprehension of our inward insight.

Precious stones Associated with Archangel Gabriel...

The fundamental gem is Amber anyway there are additionally associations with Citrine, Carnelian and Clear Quartz. This multitude of wonderful gems will elevate instinct and clean up any restricting convictions that prevent you from having confidence in yourself. I especially like clear quartz as it's expectation can be changed and adjusted relying upon what we really want assistance with. Gabriel helps us to see issues contrastingly and track down elective ways of imparting so this functions admirably for me. Anyway you might like to begin with a gem in Gabriels variety energy field to develop your relationship first.

Carnelian is especially really great for inspiration, positive life decisions, energy and boldness. It brings through Gabriels fun side and pushing you to continue onward. On the off chance that you are deficient in energy, this is a go to precious stone. In the event that you are likewise hoping to ignite thoughts and get correspondence rolling through a gathering then carnelian put in a work area or occupied piece of the home additionally functions admirably. Gabriels energy will mix into the circumstance and individuals worried to make concordance and a feeling of arranging.

Step by step instructions to Connect With Archangel Gabriel and Feel His Energy...

Gabriel has an incredibly delicate, delicate energy with sparkles of imagination and tomfoolery. To interface you simply need to ask that Gabriel enter your life and help you with a specific issue or circumstance. You might feel a breeze, see ignites or blazes of oranges.

How to Connect With Archangel Gabriel and Feel His Energy...

Gabriel has a very delicate, delicate energy with sparkles of innovativeness and tomfoolery. To interface you simply need to ask that Gabriel enter your life and help you with a specific issue or circumstance. You might feel a breeze, see starts or blazes of oranges and golds, and even feel in a real sense elevated. He will lift hands to compose and draw, showing you need to bring out from the brain all that you have been thinking on.

Gabriel can be called upon on the off chance that you really want assistance with time or finishing things promptly to deliver strain and stress. So request an augmentation or way around the issue so sensations of being overpowered can go. He is an outstanding Angel at setting aside opportunity, making minutes that out of nowhere mean you have longer and easing the heat off.

Where kids are concerned, you can request that Gabriel safeguard them and guide them. He will propose to you exhortation and answers for their consideration and prosperity. At last around correspondence and understanding each other. In the event that a kid experiences issues with discourse and learning, you can request that Gabriel help with bringing the most ideal help forward. You will detect a facilitate, a quiet and afterward new contacts approaching.

It is dependably vital to express appreciation at whatever point you request help as well. To be aware of the work that they accomplish for ourselves and the heavenly love they give. A couple of expressions of "Satisfy Archangel Gabriel, I ask that you give me direction and bring your energy into my ongoing circumstance. I offer gratitude for all that you do and will do to help me in my life".

Be Open, Pay Attention, Be Thankful.

CHAPTER NINE

Jophiel

Lead celestial host Jophiel is known as the heavenly messenger of excellence. She can send wonderful contemplations to assist you with fostering a delightful soul. Assuming you notice magnificence on the planet or get innovative thoughts that move you to make excellence, Jophiel might be close by. Jophiel can convey in various alternate ways that draw in your brain.

Getting Fresh Ideas

Jophiel frequently sends new plans to individuals. In the book "The Angels of Atlantis: Twelve Mighty Forces to Transform Your Life Forever," Stewart Pearce and Richard Crookes state: "the daylight beam of Jophiel's energy carries us to every day as a way to make new methodologies, with respect to every part of life."

Jophiel likewise may assist with tackling an issue that has been baffling you by introducing an answer, composes Diana Cooper in "Heavenly messenger Inspiration: Together, Humans and Angels Have the Power to Change the World": "At whatever point you are trapped in an issue and unexpectedly the arrangement is self-evident, one of Archangel Jophiel's holy messengers has presumably lit up your psyche."

Jophiel savors the experience of aiding individuals through the innovative strategy. Belinda Joubert writes in "Holy messenger Sense": "Jophiel assists you with keeping your brain loaded with imaginative thoughts and he imbues your inventive undertakings so the impression of God's adoration will be noticeable through your imaginative articulations."

Not exclusively will Jophiel give you thoughts for making something lovely, yet she may likewise assist you with valuing the magnificence around you. In "Holy messenger Sense," That's what joubert composes "You can perceive Jophiel through any imaginative creation which represents magnificence, truthfulness, uprightness, and every one of the characteristics of Spirit."

Defeating Negative Thoughts

Jophiel's energy frequently puts positive contemplations into individuals' psyches and assists them with fostering a propensity for positive reasoning. "Jophiel brings imperativeness, feeling, and the ability to free one's self from the jail of cynicism, or the bog of despond," compose Pearce and Crookes in "The Angels of Atlantis."

"Jophiel is the heavenly messenger to go to on the off chance that you are experiencing difficulty processing your encounters or winding up misstepping the same way over and over," composes Samantha Stevens in her book "The Seven Rays: A Universal Guide to the Archangels." "Jophiel likewise

helps the individuals who experience the ill effects of low confidence or who are the casualties of others' uninformed way of behaving."

There's a viable side to Jophiel's presence: understanding data obviously. In "The Angel Bible: The Definitive Guide to Angel Wisdom," Hazel Raven composes that Jophiel will "help you study and finish tests" and "assist you with engrossing new abilities and proposition light and astuteness to fuel your imagination."

Valuing Angelic Light

Since Archangel Jophiel leads holy messengers related with the yellow light beam, one of the mystical arrangement of holy messenger tones, individuals might see a yellow light when Jophiel is close by. In "The Seven Rays," That's what stevens composes "Jophiel's splendid yellow and orange light" is "believed to be the wellspring of motivation for specialists, essayists, researchers, and designers."

Pearce and Crookes write in "The Angels of Atlantis":

"In the event that you at any point feel an absence of joie de vivre, when your spirits are dulled by testing news, when you are met with the stunning commotion of common debasement, when you feel squeezed by the crudeness of life at the edge, or when the ghost of distress visits you, draw the yellow beam of Jophiel's energy around you, look into the profound excellence of the citrine beam, and your state of mind will consequently change."

Jophiel is the Archangel of Beauty. Jophiel assists us with adjusting pessimistic and positive feelings by assisting us with seeing the magnificence in every way. Assuming occasions in your day to day existence make them feel down, discouraged, or deadened, call upon Archangel Jophiel. Chief heavenly messenger Jophiel answers your requests with otherworldly examples that assist you with perceiving the delightful idea of your battle. Frequently, this comes as a light of the most ideal decisions you need to conquer it. You will realize your requests are replied when you notice the presence of yellow in your current circumstance.

Chief heavenly messenger Jophiel - The Archangel of Beauty

Chief heavenly messenger Jophiel, and that signifies "excellence of God," is well known as the Angel of Beauty. Jophiel is remembered to work with Christine and be a buddy of Archangel Metatron. At the point when I contact Jophiel, she provides me with the endowment of shrewdness to see the excellence in all things obviously. In difficult stretches, this can be particularly useful.

Some of the time throughout everyday life, we can neglect to see the value in the worth of battle when we permit negative contemplations to haze our psyches. Therefore, you might feel like a sculpture, frozen by your pessimistic feelings. You can undoubtedly lose lucidity in conditions such as these, whether they are unpleasant life altering situations or creative undertakings. Interfacing with Jophiel can assist you with seeing your contemplations, feelings, and conditions all the more obviously by utilizing the yellow light from her blazing Sword of Wisdom as a wellspring of enlightenment. Tuning into Jophiel's energy assists with carrying tranquility to our psyches and motivate inventive ways of assisting us with adjusting the great and the terrible.

Need to know which Archangels are helping YOU? Wish you understood what they need to say? Associate with your own Archangels through The Black Feather Intuitive at this point!

Signs and Symbols to Recognize Jophiel

The holy messenger energy shade of Jophiel is yellow. The most certain fire method for realizing that Jophiel is with you is to perceive the yellow highlights of your current circumstance. Some of the time individuals utilize yellow candles or citrine gemstones as apparatuses to interface with Jophiel. The radiance of the fire from Jophiel's sword or her Yellow Light Ray are images of the enlightenment they give to your viewpoints, feelings, and decisions.

Jophiel additionally motivates innovativeness and appreciation. Interface with Jophiel on the off chance that you feel trapped in a creative task or need to break new ground for a work project. Nonetheless, imagination and motivation can be valuable in something other than craftsmanship and work. For instance, Jophiel can assist you with accomplishing mental clearness while reading up for a test or test. Truth be told, Jophiel's energy might in fact help you while you are stepping through the exam!

The psychological lucidity from Jophiel is an extraordinary instrument to tune into the association of your viewpoints. Whether craftsmanship, work, or individual objectives, Jophiel's light assists you with turning into the best version of yourself. Moreover, this energy helps you perceive and value your most desirable characteristics an outcome.

Jophiel and the Sword of Wisdom

The Archangel Jophiel is much of the time portrayed holding a flaring blade, the "Sword of Wisdom." Some of these portrayals show Jophiel with the Flaming Sword of Wisdom monitoring the Tree of Life. This blazing sword is an image for Jophiel's capacity to slice through the deceptions of your viewpoints by enlightening the real essence of your otherworldly self. Its yellow light from the fire enlightens the truth of your circumstance. At the end of the day, Jophiel uses her sword to fight obliviousness brought about by misconception. You can shout to Jophiel on the off chance that you want assistance figuring out a perplexing circumstance, individual dynamic, or philosophical idea you are looking in your life.

Assuming you're getting a charge out of finding out about Jophiel, investigate my manual for Archangel Metatron: The Archangel of Empowerment.

Jophiel and the Yellow Light Ray

Chief heavenly messenger Jophiel's variety energy is yellow. Jophiel's Yellow Light Ray represents the edification that comes from God's insight. This light assists you with valuing the magnificence of your actual self. In doing as such, you can go with the most ideal decisions that anyone could hope to find to you and accomplish your objectives all the more promptly.

As the Archangel of Beauty, Jophiel can help you through various issues. One of the principal ways she does this is through change. Interfacing with Jophiel within the sight of the Yellow Light Ray is an extraordinary method for changing pessimistic considerations and sentiments into positive, useful ones. Since contemplations manifest as activities, supplanting terrible considerations with delightful considerations is an extraordinary initial phase in changing your battle into something rich and brilliant.

We as a whole are defied with individual difficulties. I, in the same way as other individuals, am the cause all my own problems once in a while. Notwithstanding, with Jophiel's heavenly enlightenment, I deal with my concerns with reestablished clearness and development.

Shut your eyes and interface with your breath. Essentially notice your breath entering and leaving through your noses. Feel the breath filling and discharging your lungs. Be quiet and purposeful in easing back your breath.

How to connect with Archangel Jophiel:

Breathe in... ..breathe out... ..breathe in... ... .breathe out... ... .

breathe in... ... ... breathe out. Tune in for the sound of quiet in the room. Permit yourself to be wrapped by that quietness. Permit yourself to feel light and free. You feel so light now, like you could drift like an inflatable up through the roof and very high.

As you partake in this sensation, you become mindful of another presence going along with you. It is Archangel Jophiel. As she enters your energy, she upgrades your quietness and you feel shivery and warm everywhere. Rehash without holding back this expectation: Hi Jophiel! I'm regarded to meet you! I need to get to realize you better. I'd very much want to find out about your gifts, and how you speak with me. I'm prepared to accept your direction. Kindly show me excellence and trust in the entirety of its structures in my day to day existence, in an unmistakable, obvious way now. I'm so thankful you have worked everything out!

In the event that you wish, take this time now to add an individual expectation for this examination.

Jophiel grins broadly, and leads you considerably higher out of sight, past the environment and into the general star space encompassing the Earth. At the point when you are prepared to proceed with your experience, tenderly open your eyes.

CHAPTER TEN

Ariel

Chief heavenly messenger Ariel is known as the heavenly messenger of nature. She administers the security and recuperating of creatures and plants on Earth and furthermore directs the consideration of regular components like water and wind. Ariel rouses people to take great consideration of planet Earth.

Past her job supervising nature, Ariel additionally urges individuals to satisfy God's maximum capacity for them by finding and satisfying God's motivations for their lives. Is Ariel attempting to speak with you? Here are a few indications of Ariel's presence when she is close by:

Ariel's Sign - Inspiration from Nature

Ariel's particular sign is utilizing nature to motivate individuals, adherents say. Such motivation frequently propels individuals to answer God's call to take great consideration of the regular habitat.

In her book "The Angel Blessings Kit, Revised Edition: Cards of Sacred Guidance and Inspiration," Kimberly Marooney states: "Ariel is a strong heavenly messenger of nature. ... At the point when you can perceive and value the existence inside the dirt, bushes, blossoms, trees, rocks, breezes, mountains, and oceans, you will make the way for the perception and acknowledgment of these favored ones. Request that Ariel bring you far back into the failed to remember memory of your starting point. Help the Earth by perceiving and fostering your capacity to work with nature."

Veronique Jarry writes in her book "Who Is Your Guardian Angel?" that Ariel "uncovers the main mysteries of nature. He shows stowed away fortunes."

Ariel "is benefactor of the multitude of wild creatures, and in this pretense, directs the domain of the nature spirits, like pixies, mythical people, and leprechauns, which are otherwise called nature heavenly messengers," composes Jean Barker in her book "The Angel Whispered." "Ariel and her amazing people can assist us with grasping the regular rhythms of the earth and to encounter the supernatural recuperating properties of rocks, trees, and plants. She additionally attempts to help recuperate and take care of all creatures, particularly the people who live in water."

Barker adds that Ariel at times speaks with individuals by utilizing her namesake creature: a lion (since "Ariel" signifies "lion of God"). "In the event that you see pictures or feel lions or lionesses close to you," composes Barker, "this is a sign she is with you."

Chief heavenly messenger Ariel Can Help You Reach Your Full Potential God has additionally accused Ariel of the errand of assisting individuals with arriving at their maximum capacity throughout everyday life. At the point when Ariel is attempting to assist you with being all you can be, she might uncover more about God's motivations for your life or help you with defining objectives, conquering obstructions, and accomplishing what's best for you, say devotees.

Ariel helps individuals "to recover what is best inside themselves, and in others too," composes Jarry in "Who Is Your Guardian Angel?" "He needs his protégés to have serious areas of strength for an unobtrusive brain. They will have good thoughts and brilliant considerations. They are exceptionally discerning, and their faculties will be extremely sharp. They will actually want to find new ways or have creative thoughts. These disclosures can prompt following another way in their daily routines, or making extraordinary changes in their lives."

In his book "Reference book of Angels," Richard Webster composes that Ariel "assists individuals with putting forth objectives and accomplish their aspirations."

Ariel can assist you with making a wide range of kinds of disclosures, including: "impactful discernment, mystic capacities, disclosure of stowed away fortunes, disclosure of nature's mysteries, affirmation, appreciation, nuance, prudence, conveyor of groundbreaking thoughts, creator, dramatic dreams and contemplations, perceptiveness, clairaudience, clairsentience, [and] revelation of philosophical privileged insights that lead to the reorientation of one's life," compose Kaya and Christiane Muller in their book "The Book of Angels: Dreams, Signs, Meditation: The Hidden Secrets."

In his book "The Angel Whisperer: Incredible Stories of Hope and Love from the Angels" Kyle Gray refers to Ariel as "a valiant heavenly messenger who assists us with defeating any feelings of trepidation or stresses in our way."

Barker writes in "The Angel Whispered:" "Assuming you really want boldness or certainty with the present circumstance or help with supporting your convictions, call upon Ariel, who will then tenderly yet solidly guide you to be valiant and go to bat for your convictions."

Pink Light

Seeing pink light close by may likewise make you aware of Ariel's presence since her energy relates generally to the pink light beam in the arrangement of holy messenger tones, adherents say. A key precious stone that vibrates at that equivalent energy recurrence is rose quartz, which individuals some of the time use as a device in petition to speak with God and Ariel.

In "The Angel Whispered," Barker expresses: "Ariel's quality is a pale shade of pink and her gemstone/gem is pink quartz. Ask her for what you want and she will direct you. Be that as it may, make sure to set to the side your natural assumptions, as they just cutoff what Ariel can bring into your life."

CHAPTER ELEVEN

Azrael

Azrael is the heavenly messenger of death in some Abrahamic religions, specifically Islam and a few customs of Judaism.He is likewise referred to in Sikhism.

Comparative with comparative ideas of such creatures, Azrael holds a somewhat generous job as God's heavenly messenger of death; he goes about as a psychopomp, liable for moving the spirits of the departed after their death.Both in Islam and in Judaism, he is said to hold a parchment concerning the destiny of humans, recording and eradicating their names at their introduction to the world and demise, separately.

Contingent upon the viewpoint and statutes of the different religions in which he is a figure, he may likewise be depicted as an occupant of the Third Heaven, a division of paradise in Judaism, Islam and Christianity. In Islam he is one of the four lead celestial hosts, and is related to the Quranic Malak al Mawt 'holy messenger of death'), which compares with the Hebrew-language term Mal'akh ha-Maweth in Rabbinic writing. In Hebrew, Azrael means "Heavenly messenger of God" or "Help from God".The name Azrael shows a Hebrew-language beginning, and archeological proof found in Jewish settlements in Mesopotamia affirm that it was for sure utilized in Aramaic

Incantation texts from the seventh century. However, as the text just records names, it can't be resolved whether Azrael was related with death before the coming of Islam.

After the development of Islam, the name Azrael becomes famous among both Jewish and Islamic writing, as well as legends. The name spelled as Ezrael shows up in the Ethiopic variant of Apocalypse of Peter (dating to the sixteenth 100 years) as a holy messenger of misery, who vindicates the people who had been violated during life.Along with Jibrail, Mikhail, and Israfil, Azrael is one of the four significant lead celestial hosts in Islam.He is answerable for removing the spirits of the departed from the body.Azrael doesn't act freely, yet is possibly educated by God when time really depends on take a soul.

In Quran and its exposition

Surah 32:11 notices a heavenly messenger of death related to Azrael.[14] When the unbelievers in damnation shout out for help, a heavenly messenger, likewise related to Azrael, will show up not too far off and let them know that they need to remain. Other Quranic refrains allude to a large number of heavenly messengers of death. As per analysis, these refrains allude to lesser heavenly messengers of death, subordinative to Azrael, who help the lead celestial host in his obligation. Tafsir al-Baydawi makes reference to a whole host of heavenly messengers of death, subordinative to Azrael.

A few present day contemporary like Wahbah al-Zuhayli, and researchers from Islamic University of Madinah, Indonesian strict service, Saudi Islamic issue service and Masjid al-Haram has gathered the traditional exposition from part Al-Anfal section 50 Quran 8:50, that the heavenly messenger of death has exceptional errands during the skirmish of Badr.

In Hadiths and its exposition

As per one Muslim practice, 40 days before the demise of an individual methodologies, God drops a leaf from a tree underneath the wonderful lofty position, on which Azrael peruses the name of the individual he should take with him. Al-Qurtubi described critique from traditional researcher, Ibn Zhafar al-Wa'izh, that Azrael, has a shape looking like a blue shaded smash, has various eyes in various places, and as per Ikrimah Mawla Ibn 'Abbas [id; ar], Tabi'un researcher, the size of Azrael were tremendous to such an extent that "in the event that the Earth were placed on his shoulder, it would resemble a bean in an open field".He likewise had 4,000 wings which comprised of two sorts, "wings of effortlessness" and "wings of punishment". The "wings of discipline" are produced using iron bars, snares, and scissors. Muqatil ibn Sulayman has kept his discourse in his editorial work, as-Suluk, the holy messenger had 70,000 foot limbs.

Umar ibn Abd al-Aziz, a caliph of Umayyad tradition, has detailed a portrayal that the holy messenger of death (Malak al-Mawt) has furnished with flaring whip.Caliph Umar likewise revealed a portrayal that the heavenly messenger of death was gigantic to the point that even he overshadowed Bearers of the Throne, gathering of heavenly messengers which are known as the greatest among angels.

The "Islamic Book of Dead" portrays him with 4 countenances, and his entire body comprises of eyes and tongues whose number compares to the quantity of people possessing the Earth.

Connection among Azrael and Death

Islam explained further stories concerning the connection among Azrael and Death. Christian Lange referenced that as indicated by certain researchers Azrael and Death were one element; other interpretation researchers thought Azrael and Death were various substances, with Death as some sort of hardware utilized by Azrael to take life.[31]: 129

One record clarifies passing and its connection for Azrael, addressing Death and Azrael as previous two separate elements, however when God made Death, God requested the heavenly messengers to view it and they faint for 1,000 years. After the holy messengers recaptured cognizance, Death perceived that it should submit to Azrael. The distinguishing proof of "Death" and holy messenger Azrael as one element were made sense of in a Hadith about the destiny of "Death" substance itself after the day of atonement, where traditional hanafite researcher Badr al-Din al-Ayni has deciphered in that Hadith which gathered in Sahih Bukhari assortment, that Death would assume the type of a smash, then, at that point, put among heaven and heck, lastly butchered by God himself, causing Death stop existing, which followed by God to pronounce to the two individuals of heaven and damnation that forever has started, and their state won't ever end. Lange referenced that as per a few researchers, the slam in that Hadith portrayal is no other than the holy messenger of death himself, while others declare, this to be passing's own structure in the hereafter.

In other record obtained from Muqatil ibn Sulayman, Azrael and passing were said as one element as he detailed the holy messenger has number of countenances and hands equivalent to the quantity of residing animals on his body, where every one of those appearances and hands are associated with the existence of every spirits in the residing world. Whenever a face inside Azrael body evaporated, then, at that point, the spirit which associated with it will encounter death.Furthermore, related translation from a few gatherings of current Islamic researchers from Imam Mohammad Ibn Saud Islamic University in Yemen and Mauritania has given fatwa that taken the understanding from Ibn Kathir in regards to Quran part Al-An'am stanza 61, and a hadith sent by Abu Hurairah and Ibn Abbas, that the holy messenger of death has helping holy messengers who helped him taking souls.

The eighth Umayyad Caliph Umar ibn Abd al-Aziz once detailed the editorial viewing Azrael in Quran section As-Sajdah refrain 11 Quran 32:11, that taking many lives are exceptionally simple for the holy messenger, that as would be natural for caliph "maybe the whole humankind on earth were just similar to dish on the plate according to the viewpoint of Malak al-Mawt (holy messenger of death)". Meanwhile, Al-Qurtubi has described from the power of Mujahid ibn Jabr that the world being between the hands of the Angel of Death is "like a vessel between the hands of a human; he assumes from anything that position he needs", where Mujahid portrayed that Azrael can jump all over numerous spirits at a similar opportunity since God made the earth contracted for him until maybe it is a vessel between his hands. A comparative Marfu' Hadith (i.e., with a raised chain of transmission) was accounted for by Zuhayr ibn Muhammad.

In fables

Azrael kept his significance in daily existence. As per the Sufi educator Al-Jili, Azrael appears to the spirit in a structure given by its most remarkable representations. A typical conviction holds that the lesser heavenly messengers of death are for the everyday citizens, while holy people and prophets meet the lead celestial host of death himself.Great prophets, for example, Moses and

Muhammad are welcomed graciously by him, however holy people are likewise said to meet Azrael in lovely structures. It is said that, when Rumi was going to pass on, he laid in his bed and met Azrael in human shape. The conviction that Azrael seems to holy people before they really kick the bucket to set themselves up for death, is likewise confirmed by the confirmation of Nasir Khusraw, in which he professes to have met Azrael during his rest, illuminating him about his impending death.

As per one more renowned account which recorded by Ibn Kathir in his work, Qishaash al-Anbiya (story of the prophets), God once requested Gabriel, Mikael, Israfil, and Azrael to gather dust from earth from which Adam should be made. Just Azrael succeeded, whereupon he was bound to turn into the holy messenger concerning life and passing of humanity.

Western gathering

The Islamic idea of Azrael, including a few stories, for example, the story of Solomon, a hadith arriving at back to Shahr Ibn Hawshab, was at that point known in America in the eighteenth 100 years as verified by Gregory Sharpe and James Harris.

A few Western adaptions broadened the actual portrayal of Azrael, thus the writer Leigh Hunt portrays Azrael as wearing a dark hooded shroud. Albeit coming up short on the prominent sickle, his depiction in any case looks like the Grim Reaper.Henry Wadsworth Longfellow specifies Azrael in The Reaper and the Flowers as a holy messenger of death, however he isn't compared with Samael, the heavenly messenger of death in Jewish legend who shows up as a fallen and vindictive heavenly messenger, instead.[39] Azrael likewise shows up in G. K. Chesterton's sonnet "Lepanto" as one of the Islamic spirits directed by

"Mahound" (Muhammad) to oppose Don John of Austria's campaign. In the Smurfs, the feline of the shrewd wizard Gargamel is called Azrael.

I see Archangel Azrael as a brilliant partner whose presence makes everything okay. He carries with him a feeling of quiet that can light up the core of a lamenting soul. I feel a specific warmth, solace and security at whatever point the Archangel Azrael is around me. He remains close by as a faithful protector assisting me with traveling through my sadness, acknowledge what is, push ahead and opt for joy.

This superb chief heavenly messenger is loaded up with mending light prepared to direct the people who are encountering heartbreaks because of the passing of a friend or family member, a fantasy, a task, a relationship, or anything that brings you into a condition of misfortune.

In Hebrew, Archangel Azrael means 'Heavenly messenger of God'. He is known as the Angel of Grief. Among every one of the Archangels, Archangel Azrael is the most un-known and frequently one of the most misjudged.

Since Archangel Azrael is otherwise called the 'Holy messenger of Death', many individuals dread him - thinking he brings demise. Be that as it may, this isn't true. All things being equal, Archangel Azrael helps those lamenting the departure of a friend or family member arrange their lives.

Other than aiding those lamenting, he helps the individuals who are changing from the actual domain to the soul world. It's the obligation of Archangel Azrael to assist the leaving soul with segregating from the actual body and move over to their next period of life in the great beyond. He comforts biting the dust spirits and helps them through seven magnificent lobbies. The excursion through these seven planetary circles permits the departed to audit their life. Spirits going through this cycle have an opportunity to ponder the activities they took when they lived in the actual structure; mend their injuries and get ready for their next section.

Chief heavenly messenger Azrael is likewise answerable for monitoring all the withdrawing spirits and checking their rebirth.

Need to know which Archangels are helping YOU? Wish you understood what they need to say? Interface with your own Archangels through The Black Feather Intuitive at this point!

Traveling Through Grief with Archangel Azrael

For most people, confronting the feeling of misery is perhaps of the most difficult and overwhelming experience we can have. It appears to be hard, frequently somewhat incomprehensible, to go through the deficiency of somebody dear to heart whether through death, division, or migration. Simply the prospect of losing something we hold dear can cause pressure.

We lament since we would rather not acknowledge the change. We become so sincerely connected to individuals and things that even a slight change is difficult to adapt to. At the point when we lose a person or thing, we would rather not register the way that the individual or thing is gone from our everyday lives, in how we were accustomed to encountering them, until the end of time. This causes misery, and makes our heart weighty with the misfortune.

The sorrow interaction can be separated into seven phases:

Shock - Where the individual encounters powerlessness and loss of motion hearing the terrible news

Refusal - Where the individual attempts to keep away from the circumstance

Outrage - Where the individual has explosions (or "in-explodes") of stifled feelings

Haggling - Where the individual searches an exit from the circumstance

Despondency - Where the individual understands what is going on or the misfortune and its profound load prevents them from unreservedly carrying on with their life

Testing - Where the individual searches for answers for emerge from the sorrow

Acknowledgment - Where the individual at long last searches for a method for continuing on the presence of Archangel Azrael helps both the withering, as well as individuals associated with them, to assist them with tracking down solace and harmony in the interim.

Albeit, previously, Azrael has principally worked with spirits progressing from the actual world into the soul aspect, he is currently stepping in to open the door for general recuperating energy, solace, and love to individuals abandoned who are grieving the deficiency of somebody close. This heavenly messenger emanates with insight and compassion, directing individuals on the best way to manage the flight of a spirit. He attempts to retain all aggravation to ease up the hearts of those in grieving, and shares his insight to tell them the best way to embrace their new situation in a delicate, cherishing way.

Other than aiding all spirits on the move, and their excess friends and family, the Archangel Azrael additionally directs experts who are associated with setting up the perishing like attendants, ministry, and hospice laborers.

Assuming you're getting a charge out of finding out about Azrael, investigate my manual for Archangel Jeremiel: The Archangel of Forgiveness.

The Archangel Azrael is portrayed as a winged man in a smooth white robe.

Some partner the Archangel as a light emission smooth light that is loaded up with adoration, insight, and solace. For my purposes, Azrael is a heavenly light that ingests my distresses and despondency and helps me "maintain some kind of control" when my spirit is hurting.

Azrael and the White Energy

The white energy of Azrael brings recuperating while at the same time taking the distress of individuals who call upon him. I frequently envision this velvety white light unobtrusively overwhelming our pain and making up for the shortcoming in our heart with a feeling of sympathy, consolation, and solace. This white light is likewise a sign that the withdrew soul finds a sense of contentment.

Azrael and Yellow Calcite Crystal Healing

Azrael is the Archangel of second beam. In this way, the lead celestial host is associated with unrestricted love, astuteness, and direction.

Mystics and mediums frequently utilize Yellow Calcite to interface with this astral light since the gem is related with trust and fearlessness. The gemstone is utilized to get out old energy examples and improve inspiration and drive. These properties make Yellow Calcite helpful for the people who are fighting grief and agony because of the deficiency of somebody darling.

Shut your eyes and associate with your breath. Breathe in and breathe out leisurely and profoundly multiple times, permitting your breath to fill your whole body from head to toe.

You are feeling warm and agreeable. Envision that you are strolling gradually along a stone way. The way is loaded up with wonderful white and clear quartz precious stones. With each step, you feel a shivering sensation ascending through your feet, calves, and thighs, filling your mid-region and chest cavity, your arms, shoulders, neck, and head. You are partaking in this high-recurrence walk.

The gem way in the long run leads you into an exquisite, tranquil blossom garden, loaded up with splendid tropical varieties. Hummingbirds, honey bees and butterflies dance around each other in a celebration of nectar and honey. Splendid lavish trees sprinkle the sky blue sky.

As you investigate this fragrant nursery, contacting petals and leaves of silk, velvet, and papyrus, you notice the way prompts a gurgling, clear freshwater creek with a scaffold.

This lavish scaffold is apparently made of light, as the sun shines off the precious stone base, with a delightfully fashioned iron railing. In the middle, sits a seat, shrouded in indigo and purple morning wonders. You stroll onto the extension and plunk down on this seat, taking in the Close your eyes and associate with your breath. Breathe in and breathe out leisurely and profoundly multiple times, permitting your breath to fill your whole body from head to toe.

You are feeling warm and agreeable. Envision that you are strolling gradually along a stone way. The way is loaded up with delightful white and clear quartz precious stones. With each step, you feel a shivering sensation ascending through your feet, calves, and thighs, filling your midsection and chest pit, your arms, shoulders, neck, and head. You are partaking in this high-recurrence walk.

CHAPTER TWELVE

Chamuel

At the point when I feel like a relationship with a companion or cherished one is enduring, Archangel Chamuel assists me with moving a tranquil way to deal with tackling anything that issues are causing struggle. Chamuel, whose name signifies "one who looks for God," is the Archangel of Peace. He essentially utilizes his heavenly powers to assist with peopling foster harmony with themselves and with others by assisting them with moving toward their concerns with adoration and sympathy.

There are times in life when we could feel unfriendly or angry. Thus, we can attack others or hold onto pessimistic inclinations toward the world. As such, these are times when we are not settled. This uncertainty in ourselves is what we wind up producing to the world, and accordingly what we feel from the world. Everybody feels like they have foes now and again, and frequently the wellspring of our negative discernment is really established in ourselves.

You could recall when you had a battle with a friend or family member, or unreasonably passed judgment on somebody. This is a piece of life. Be that as it may, every one of these minutes present significant chances to find out about ourselves and our general surroundings. Maybe you've been blasted with a thought on the most proficient method to determine one of these issues, or how to work on a significant relationship or fellowship. This motivation is crafted by Chamuel. He assists us with developing the individual harmony that we want for relational harmony. All things considered, tranquil associations with others starts with a serene relationship with yourself. Let Archangel Chamuel be your manual for adoring, serene connections!

Chief heavenly messenger Chamuel - The Archangel of Peace

Harmony is an intriguing idea that can be surprisingly convoluted on a superficial level. What motivates it? What keeps up with it? It is essential to understand that generally, when individuals act adversely towards others, it is an impression of how they treat themselves. Lead celestial host Chamuel assists us with perceiving this propensity in ourselves and others. At the point when we can comprehend the reason why there is unrest in our internal identities or connections, we can move toward them with empathy as opposed to judgment.

In any case, the harmony that Chamuel motivates isn't generally essentially a method for tackling a contention. As a matter of fact, discovering a true sense of harmony inside ourselves is critical to finding the certainty that permits us to cultivate new fellowships or coexist better with partners. These connections may be enduring on the off chance that somebody feels that they are not worth a lot, or on the other hand on the off chance that they just miss the mark on certainty to straightforwardly draw in with others. These gloomy feelings that lead to low confidence or low self-esteem are everything except serene. By motivating internal harmony, Chamuel assists individuals with building certainty, confidence, and self-pardoning.

Need to know which Archangels are helping YOU? Wish you understood what they need to say? Interface with your own Archangels through The Black Feather Intuitive at this point!

The most effective method to Recognize Archangel Chamuel

Chief heavenly messenger Chamuel is in many cases portrayed in workmanship with hearts. Hearts are generally representative of adoration, which is Chamuel's most prominent device. By motivating adoration in the people who call upon him, Chamuel permits individuals to foster more grounded, further associations with others around them and themselves.

One more certain fire method for realizing that Chamuel is with you is to search for pink in your current circumstance. You could see pink light or notice pink articles around you. You can rely on seeing this tone as an indication of Chamuel's Pink Light Ray, his heavenly energy.

Chamuel and the Pink Light Ray

As the Archangel of Peace, Chamuel's energy tone is pink. Chamuel's Pink Light Ray typifies the heavenly love that he moves in the people who call upon him. The Pink Light Ray assists us treat ourselves with affection, which permits us to effortlessly act with adoration to individuals around us more.

There are numerous ways that Chamuel utilizes his Pink Light Ray to assist us with various issues. Calling upon Archangel Chamuel within the sight of this light beam is an optimal method for starting changing our connections. By zeroing in on this heavenly energy source, you can change your pessimistic sentiments into positive ones. The main piece of this change is love, and likewise, empathy.

Chief heavenly messenger Chamuel and Relationships

Chief heavenly messenger Chamuel is most popular for his powers in assisting individuals with their connections. These can be heartfelt, cordial, or expert. He likewise assists individuals keep a solid relationship with themselves. At the point when you feel like you want assistance keeping up with sound relations with individuals around you, Chamuel is there to help! He helps individuals mostly by permitting individuals to embrace caring ways to deal with their concerns. Through the cherishing and humane comprehension of Chamuel, you can rehearse absolution and useful activity.

This could try and assist with peopling find their perfect partners! With Archangel Chamuel as their aide, individuals approach others with adoration and sympathy. This eventually permits them to be available to new individuals. Some of the time we track down affection in surprising spots, and some of the time that implies allowing individuals the opportunity to show you who they truly are. Thus, we sidestep shallow parts of individuals and look rather at their internal being. That is the reason they're designated "perfect partners"!

Chief heavenly messenger Chamuel is the lead celestial host of adoration and harmony. His name signifies 'the person who looks for God', however there is such a lot of that this lead celestial host can assist us with. He is perceived all through the world, taking various names in various religions.

Assuming that you are needing assistance with connections and agreement, Archangel Chamuel can help you. This strong being can direct us throughout everyday life, and in this article, I need to go through every one of the astonishing parts of Archangel Chamuel.

We will realize what his identity is, the way to remember him, and how to associate with him when we are out of luck. Lead celestial host Chamuel is the chief heavenly messenger of serene connections and concordance. He helps those discover a genuine sense of reconciliation, both with themselves and everyone around them. He gives you the solidarity to defeat tough spots, tracking down clearness and understanding when required.

The chief heavenly messenger of sympathy and care, there is a great deal we can gain from Archangel Chamuel. By associating with him, we can better ourselves and how we act to others in our lives.

He helps us in excusing those that enjoy hurt us and tracking down harmony inside. By working with Archangel Chamuel, we can foster serene and cherishing associations with those around us.When we are fostering a relationship with our twin fire, it can likewise be truly helpful to interface with Archangel Chamuel. He can direct us in making a satisfying and agreeable union.It can be challenging to perceive Archangel Chamuel from the start, and this is on the grounds that we may not be knowing what to search for. Since holy messengers exist on a higher vibrational recurrence, they are seldom seen in their actual structure in the actual world.However, lead celestial hosts are dependably there in the universe, and we simply have to open up our spirits to them. By knowing what to search for to perceive Archangel Chamuel, we can facilitate our association with him.

Anyway, what are what to pay special attention to while needing to perceive Archangel Chamuel?

Chief heavenly messenger CHAMUEL SYMBOL

Since the Archangel Chamuel is the chief heavenly messenger of affection and harmony, his most huge heavenly messenger image is the heart. Assuming you are seeing heart shapes spotted in your general surroundings, you realize that he is close.

He is additionally connected with the image of the pigeon. The pigeon experiences long been related with harmony and subsequently interfaces with the Archangel Chamuel.ARCHANGEL CHAMUEL NUMBER

Lead celestial host Chamuel is connected to the number 7. This number areas of strength for has of otherworldly arousing, love, and karma. It is an unbelievably strong number, addressing completion and achievement throughout everyday life.

The number 7 reminds us to be smart and mindful in all parts of our lives.

Seeing the heavenly messenger numbers 77, 777, and 7777 all recommend that Archangel Chamuel is close by.

Chief heavenly messenger CHAMUEL COLOR

All chief heavenly messengers are connected to explicit holy messenger tones. Chief heavenly messenger Chamuel is connected to pink, as this tone major areas of strength for has of affection and harmony.If you are seeing a light pink tone around you, this is on the grounds that Archangel Chamuel is close by and prepared to help you.

This variety connects to the heart chakra, which permits you to open up to cherish and tranquil connections. While needing to work with both Archangel Chamuel and your heart chakra, encircling yourself with pink candles and crystals is really useful. These will emit explicit vibrations that interface you with the chief heavenly messenger of adoration.

HOW TO CONNECT WITH ARCHANGEL CHAMUEL?

All chief heavenly messengers are there to help us on our way throughout everyday life. Be that as it may, it can now and again be difficult to interface with them, particularly assuming we have never done it before.So, I need to go through the most effective ways of associating with Archangel Chamuel. Nonetheless, it is vital to recall that it requires investment and practice to interface with the chief heavenly messengers. In any case, don't surrender - they are in that frame of mind to help and guide you.

Contemplation

Contemplation is one of the most amazing ways of associating with Archangel Chamuel. By focusing yourself and interesting to him, you are making the way for help from Archangel Chamuel.When I need to interface with Archangel Chamuel through reflection, I will light a pink candle. This is on the grounds that he is connected to pink and it gives forward vibrations of adoration and harmony.

Here is a contemplation custom that will permit you to interface with Archangel Chamuel:

Track down your place of refuge, away from whatever might upset you. Sit serenely either on the floor or on a seat. Pause for a minute to rest, permitting considerations to go all through your brain uninhibitedly.

Shut your eyes and spotlight on your breath. Breathe in through your nose and breathe out through your mouth, permitting energy to course through you. It is OK to allow your psyche to meander as of now. Simply ensure you get energy streaming and development in your spirit.

At the point when you have focused yourself, picture a pink sphere of light on your chest. Envision a little light, brimming with potential. Permit it to associate with your heart chakra and the feelings you are feeling.

Gradually imagine the pink circle developing, spreading over your body. Envision the pink light encompassing you, embracing your entire body. As you are doing as such, continue breathing profoundly. In through your nose and out through your mouth.

Whenever you are absorbed the pink light, the time has come to direct your concentration toward Archangel Chamuel. Request that he come to you. You can do this either in your mind or without holding back. It ultimately depends on you what you say, however basically, 'I request that Archangel Chamuel help me' will stand out enough to be noticed!

Assuming you need, you can request something explicit from Archangel Chamuel. On the off chance that you are experiencing issues with a relationship, right now is an ideal opportunity to tell him.

Gems

Precious stones are an extraordinary approach to interfacing with Archangel Chamuel. This is on the grounds that he knows about the energy of specific precious stones and will see you utilizing them.

Chief heavenly messenger Chamuel is connected to pink quartz, which has vibrations of adoration, delicacy, and care. It is additionally connected to the heart chakra and the number 7. By utilizing pink quartz, we can acknowledge unqualified love and backing into our lives, excusing and failing to remember the people who have harmed us.

One more gem that can be utilized to associate with Archangel Chamuel is green fluorite. This is areas of strength for a stone that permits you to conquer profound torment and sorrow. It is connected to the heart chakra and has purifying and quieting energy.

SHOW UNCONDITIONAL LOVE AND SUPPORT

One manner by which we can interface with lead celestial hosts is by showing their characteristics and convictions. Thus, assuming you are needing to associate with Archangel Chamuel, it is valuable to chip away at how you act toward people around you.

Have you dropped out with a companion as of late? Do you not address somebody significant in that frame of mind however much you used to? Right now is an ideal opportunity to change this. Contact that companion who you have had a contention with! Show them unrestricted love and work on having a serene and amicable relationship with them.

Does anybody in your life require support at the present time? How might you help them? Think about where you are at this moment and how you collaborate with those less lucky than you. Have a contemplate on the off chance that there is anything you can do to facilitate their aggravation.

Look at YOUR OWN THOUGHT PROCESSES

Chief heavenly messenger Chamuel is the lead celestial host of adoration and harmony. This actually intends that assuming you spread energy of affection and harmony, he will be simpler to associate with.

Along these lines, to truly interface with Chamuel looking at your own manners of thinking is really significant. Is it safe to say that you are showing adoration, light, and harmony at this moment?

Invest energy looking at your viewpoints and convictions, distinguishing any areas of outrage and disdain. How might you change these?

chief heavenly messenger chamuel petition

It very well might be really smart to rehearse shadow work while needing to free yourself of outrage and agony. Shadow work can assist you with distinguishing any negative behavior patterns in your manners of thinking, permitting you to relinquish convictions and thoughts that don't serve you.

I won't lie, this sort of training requires some investment! You can't just change your negative points of view straight away. However, with care, shadow work, and understanding, we can set ourselves free from negative considerations.

PRACTICE SELF-LOVE AND GRATITUDE

Heard the expression, 'you can't cherish anybody except if you love yourself first'? Indeed, I think there is a reality to this. Thus, when we are needing to interface with Archangel Chamuel and manifest his characteristics, we should deal with ourselves and practice self esteem.

By rehearsing confidence, we are conveying positive energy into the universe for Archangel Chamuel to answer.

All in all, what's the significance here to rehearse self esteem?!

Indeed, a decent spot to start is through sure certifications. By rehashing positive self esteem insistences consistently, we are figuring out how to acknowledge ourselves and what our identity is. I likewise am a major devotee to appreciation, and have an appreciation diary that I write in many days!

By adding confidence and appreciation into our everyday daily practice, we are welcoming positive energy into our lives.

Lead celestial host CHAMUEL PRAYER

Imploring Archangel Chamuel is an incredible method for interfacing with him. By addressing him straightforwardly, you are permitting him to enter your life. He will hear the request and help you.

The following are a couple of petitions for Archangel Chamuel.

A PRAYER FOR FORGIVENESS

At the point when I need to pardon somebody in my life and beat issues in relational connections, I will continuously go to Archangel Chamuel.

Here is a request to Archangel Chamuel that permits pardoning

Dear Archangel Chamuel, I request your direction. If it's not too much trouble, permit me to excuse those that have harmed me, and furnish me with just love in my heart. Allow me to gain from you to acquire harmony and love.

A PRAYER FOR LOVE

Here is an overall supplication to permit love into your life and heart.

Dear Archangel Chamuel, I request your energy and love. If it's not too much trouble, send forward your energy into my heart and permit me to embrace all the adoration in my life. Much thanks to you for your unqualified direction and backing.

A PRAYER FOR PEACE

Lead celestial host Chamuel is the heavenly messenger of harmony, and we can engage him when we need to discover a sense of reconciliation in our own lives.